LONDON

LONDON

A GUIDE TO RECENT ARCHITECTURE / SAMANTHA HARDINGHAM

BATSFORD

BRITISH LIBRARY CATALOGUING IN PUBLICATION
A CIP RECORD FOR THIS BOOK IS AVAILABLE FROM THE BRITISH LIBRARY

PUBLISHED BY B T BATSFORD
64 BREWERY ROAD, LONDON N7 9NT
WWW.BATSFORD.COM
SERIES EDITOR TOM NEVILLE
SERIES DESIGN CLAUDIA SCHENK

FIRST PUBLISHED 2002
COPYRIGHT © 2002 B T BATSFORD, A member of Chrysalis Books plc

ISBN 0 7134 8806 9

PRINTING AND BINDING IN ITALY

FOR A COPY OF THE BATSFORD CATALOGUE OR INFORMATION
ON SPECIAL QUANTITY ORDERS OF BATSFORD BOOKS PLEASE
CONTACT US ON 020 7697 3000 OR SALES@CHRYSALISBOOKS.CO.UK

Samantha Hardingham 2003

CONTENTS

INTRODUCTION

This guide contains descriptions of more than 100 built projects which provide an up-to-date record of London's most recent architecture. The aim of the book is to initiate an architectural tour, pointing out some of the latest building types and techniques along the way. Although projects are discussed individually, it is important to view each one in the larger context of the city. The gaps will be filled in by your own observations.

The guide aims to maintain a very current picture, so the content has changed considerably since the first edition, written in 1993. With the arrival of the new millennium the process of architectural evolution has picked up an even brisker pace. Many of the themes outlined in the first edition reflected the events surrounding the building boom of the 1980s and the dominant postmodern style. These concerns have on the whole been superceded by a new wave of development largely encouraged by funds from the National Lottery. However, many of the buildings from that earlier period are still relevant to an understanding of the city's evolution and therefore remain in the guide. Similarly a brief description of the political climate, then and now, is vital to an understanding of why London looks the way it does today.

Between 1979 and 1997 Britain was in the hands of a Conservative government. In the early 1980s Prime Minister Margaret Thatcher initiated the deregulation of the public services that provided the essential infrastructure of the country. The lifting of state control was supposed to promote competition and, as a result, produce better services. Railways, telecommunications, water, gas, electricity, prisons, prison security and bus services are just some of the public functions that have been wholly or partly privatised. In 1986 the Labour-run Greater London Council (GLC) was abolished and the single voice that spoke for the whole city was replaced by the many voices of the individual London boroughs and numerous bodies with areas of special interest. During this era there was a dearth of new public housing (which continues today) but a simultaneous building boom in the City of London and Docklands. British and North American developers took the opportunity to build vast amounts of office space (providing all the services necessary for computerised trading) and luxury housing to accommodate well-paid employees. Concrete- or steel-framed buildings with granite cladding, sporting pop-classical motifs were quick to construct and provided an instant grandiose façade for any tenant.

The return of a Labour government in 1997 seemed to offer the chance for new policy making with a social agenda. Alarmingly, there has been little to distinguish the policies of either party; New Labour has pursued privatisation and public housing has largely been handed over to independently managed housing associations (the number of affordable homes being built has fallen to its lowest level since records began in 1949 and by almost one third since New Labour took office – according to *The Architects' Journal* in January 2003). The Peabody Trust is at the forefront of any significant housing development, particularly in its pursuit of prefabrication in their new-build schemes (see pages 232–234 and 246–250). Advisory boards such as the Royal Fine Arts Commission have been turned into the Commission for Architecture and the Built Environment (CABE) and Lord Rogers became the leader of the government's Urban Task Force.

However, 2000 saw the reintroduction of a Greater London Authority and the election of Ken Livingstone as Mayor. With no political powers to speak of, just those to raise and debate issues, it seems that Livingstone's legacy will not be his headquarters near Tower Bridge and the barren 'cityscape' which is evolving around it (see pages 100–102), but the central London Congestion Charge, introduced in February 2003. Cars are excluded from the city centre during weekdays. Any car crossing the boundary is photographed and fined for the transgression. The scheme can only give impetus to the social division between the wealthy and the poor in the capital. The cost for the countless small businesses that make the city tick may be great.

To some extent a building boom continues, but now largely under the auspices of the National Lottery. The launch of the Lottery in 1994 has had a tremendous impact on London, enabling a new kind of architectural patronage to emerge. Funds from the scheme have been fed into four bodies – the Department of National Heritage, the Arts Council Lottery Fund, the Sports Council and the Millennium Commission – all of which receive proposals for new schemes. As well as local projects such as Sadler's Wells Theatre (pages 166–168) and the Jerwood Space (pages 134–136), key developments such as the Greenwich Millennium Dome (page 310) and the Royal Opera House (pages 80–84) and the link provided by the Jubilee Line Extension (pages 310–318) have opened up a whole section of London south of the Thames, and act as a catalysts for regeneration in previously neglected areas such as Southwark and Bermondsey. Some impact is beginning to be felt for instance in the shape of the Laban Dance Centre, Deptford (page 140).

Historically London's working-class area, much of the East End has been allowed to deteriorate and is now among the most poverty-stricken parts of the country, particularly since the decline of industry in Docklands. The concentration of new development at Canary Wharf has reinforced social and economic divides. More recently an attempt has been made to redress the balance and readdress the needs of local communities through the provision of medical centres, schools and youth clubs alongside the migration eastwards of artists and small businesses who cannot afford central London rates. These kinds of projects have provided opportunities for younger architectural practices, who have worked on both quick-build schemes and local landmark buildings – often with challenging briefs and budgets – and produced a variety of building types and styles as a

direct response to advances in materials technology rather than to trends or images. Plasma Studios, voted best new practice of 2002, built its first project for a jeweller in London Fields. (See also the Geffrye Museum, pages 236–238; White Cube, page 186; the handbag shop in Retford Street, page 240; and Thames Barrier Park, pages 290–292.)

Grand projects such as the Great Court at the British Museum (pages 176–178), Tate Modern (pages 120–124) and the re-opening of Somerset House in Aldwych have given London new cultural foundations on a scale not seen here since the Victorian era. These buildings create vast covered areas (appropriate for the unpredicatable British climate) simply for the pleasure of the spaces themselves, while they also lie adjacent to some of our greatest cultural resources – collections of modern art, ancient artefacts or books.

Tall buildings are on London's agenda for the immediate future; as well as the group at Canary Wharf, Norman Foster & Partner's 40-storey Swiss Re Building (see page 9), although still under construction, is already the focal point of what is rapidly becoming a cluster of skyscrapers in the financial centre. Renzo Piano's proposed tower at London Bridge (yet to gain planning permission) seeks to overshadow Foster's tower.

The Jubilee Line Extension, which opened in 2000, remains London's pre-eminent contemporary architectural expression. But the opening up of the entire south bank of the Thames for pedestrians between the Design Museum at Bermondsey up to Westminster Bridge, with new pedestrian bridges at Bankside (see Millennium Bridge, pages 126–128) linking to St Paul's cathedral, and at Charing Cross (see Hungerford Bridge, page 88), connecting to the recently pedestrianised Trafalgar Square, creates new possibilities for another change in the way we behave in London.

USING THIS BOOK

The guide is divided into ten sections, nine of which define areas of London where there are buildings of interest, and with one dedicated to the Jubilee Line extension. Some sections have been stretched to take in exceptional but isolated buildings such as the Crystal Palace concert platform in the deep south. Most of the inner London sections can be covered on foot. Public transport details are listed under each entry. For mainline rail enquiries call 0845 748 4950 or go to www.railtrack.co.uk.

If you want to read more about any of the buildings, the architects or this particular era, visit the library at the Royal Institute of British Architects, Portland Place, London W1 (020 7580 5533; check opening hours and the fee situation before you go). All the periodicals here are well catalogued and there are special files on major projects. The library can also be accessed via the internet at www.architecture.com.

ACKNOWLEDGEMENTS

Thank you to all the architectural practices for providing me with information at an increasingly efficient rate – which certainly says something about the way offices are run these days – and to all the job architects for filling in the detail. Special thanks to Bert and Freda whose view of site visits is, by their very nature, always different to my own, and to Willy for providing what he insists is 'useless information', but which proves time and again to be invaluable.

SH, January 2003

WEST AND SOUTH-WEST LONDON

1 EEL PIE ISLAND

Strictly private property, but what is visible from the footbridge (the only way on to the island), and from the path behind the house gives a good indication of what this house is made of, and what a good excuse it gives me to lure you to this most unusual backwater.

The island is both gritty and fantastical. A working boatyard, artists' and inventors' workshops and gingerbread houses reside together under the planning restriction that nothing is built above one storey. Made from the carcass of a shed on the site, No. 1 feels very much like a houseboat in dry dock. The architect rebuilt the shell with a new steel frame to support the roof. The roof has been lifted to create a clerestory window around the perimeter of the house, letting natural light into the open plan. The roof slopes in three alternating diagonals, alluding to a pitch outline as desired by the planners.

Water, a key factor in this neighbourhood (and the client is a bachelor), prompted the architects to put the bath at the centre of the plan. While lying in the tub the client has a pleasant view across the main living space, through a large plate-glass sliding door, on to decking and the river floating by. A curved wall bisects the plan diagonally to conceal bathroom pipework (and including a window opening to maintain the unobstructed view) and extends to screen a small kitchen. A bedroom is tucked away at the back of the plan.

No excuses are necessary for a low budget or a lived-in appearance – above all this is a romantic house in an enchanting place. Such things are precious in a time like this.

ADDRESS 1 Eel Pie Island, Twickenham
CLIENT Maxwell Balfour
CONTRACT VALUE £75,000
RAIL Twickenham
ACCESS none

Boyarsky Murphy Architects 2000

BROOKE COOMBES HOUSE

This four-bedroom house was designed so that construction could be undertaken by the clients themselves. The plan for this low-energy villa subverts the traditional front/back relationship of the other houses on the street. The site is broken down into strips stretching from the street to the rear wall. All accommodation is placed to one side with a continuous garden running alongside. Where it passes by the house the green space is enclosed in glass to create a double-height courtyard entrance. The wall between house and courtyard is also fully glazed to allow views into the courtyard. It can be opened up in warm weather to increase airflow and habitable space. In cold weather it acts as triple glazing.

The main structure comprises a steel frame wrapped in timber studs lined with 'Warmcell' (recycled newspaper) insulation and clad in a rainscreen of clay tiles. Windows are galvanised aluminium with double glazing. The roof is made from a composite of steel and masonite beams with a stainless-steel covering. It hovers above the shell, allowing light into all sides of the house through clerestory glazing. Rainwater is collected in ponds at the front and back of the building, and flows between the house and courtyard through a narrow channel creating enough humidity for plant growth. Any additional grey water is recirculated to flush WCs.

ADDRESS Mountfield Road, Ealing, London W5
CLIENTS John Brooke and Carol Coombes
STRUCTURAL ENGINEER Elliott Wood Partnership
SERVICES ENGINEER Max Fordham & Partners
TUBE Ealing Broadway – Central, District Lines
ACCESS although visible from the street, this is a private home so please respect the occupants' right to privacy

Burd Haward Marston Architects 2000

CHISWICK PARK

Chiswick Park is the offspring of Stockley Park, near Heathrow, the ground-breaking out-of-town business park development of the 1980s, also by Stanhope plc. This introduced a radical approach to such schemes, specifically in landscaping and in commissioning buildings designed by a range of leading architects with the aim of developing first-rate fully serviced office space rather than a no-man's land of light-industrial sheds.

Six of a proposed 12 buildings on the Chiswick Park site are complete. All follow the same four-storey model and share a design concept: 'traditional served-and-servant office space' – services run through a central core, horizontally below raised floors and a service zone under concrete slabs, with plant located on the roofs and in undercroft areas. Atria form the entrances to each building, bringing light into the centre of the plans.

In response to the parkland setting, RRP's buildings choose not to wear their services on their sleeves. The mood is tranquil: a primary concrete shell structure is encased in an external steel framework supporting a brise-soleil, cleaning gantries and an impressive array of escape stairs tied back to the primary structure by tensioned cable-stays.

Each building has its own car-parking undercroft accessed from the perimeter of the site, leaving the centre of the development free to be over-run by a naturalistic lake and river formation, bordered by a wooden boardwalk on either side, that forges its way between the outcrops of new buildings.

ADDRESS Chiswick High Road, London W4
LANDSCAPE ARCHITECT W8 Landscape Architects & Urban Planners
STRUCTURAL ENGINEER Arup
TUBE Gunnersbury/Chiswick Park – District Line
ACCESS public areas are open; restricted in office buildings

Richard Rogers Partnership 1999–2004

WEST AND SOUTH-WEST LONDON

DOCTORS' SURGERY

For a patient, a building for health located in the middle of a traffic interchange is an appalling notion. But what better place for an architect to make a first foray into new-build and prove the value of the profession than a hostile site strangled by a flyover and with faceless 1990s' offices as neighbours? There can be no argument from planners that any new building should try to 'blend in'. In fact the authority's only requirement was for a landmark building to house four doctors and a healthcare trust.

The site suggested an inward-looking plan to shield against noise and pollution and to create a series of views within the building of its own quiet space. The two-storey building is curved in plan with the north-facing wall on the road side made up of an armour of double-curved shells coated in white render. Prickly bushes have been planted around the perimeter to deter anyone tempted to put their signature on these invitingly blank canvases. The gaps between each section are glazed to admit natural light to waiting areas and the main access corridor leading to all treatment rooms. The windows are set back and angled to avoid water staining. Locating the main circulation route against this outside wall provides another layer of sound proofing between patients and traffic. The fully glazed south-facing wall overlooks an internal courtyard and is shaded by the overhang of a copper roof.

ADDRESS Hammersmith Bridge Road, London W6
CLIENT London Borough of Hammersmith & Fulham
STRUCTURAL ENGINEER Cooper Associates
CONTRACT VALUE £1.16 million **SIZE** 799 square metres
TUBE Hammersmith – District, Hammersmith & City, Piccadilly Lines
ACCESS restricted

Guy Greenfield Architects 2000

CHELSEA AND WESTMINSTER HOSPITAL

Following the closure of Westminster Hospital in Horseferry Road, this hospital embodies a government scheme to amalgamate many of London's hospitals, providing fewer beds for complex cases and leaving the rest to attend 'Super Health Centres' which I'm afraid don't actually exist yet (well, not in every community). Chelsea and Westminster Hospital provides 666 beds, clinical, research and teaching facilities, on-site accommodation for approximately 300 staff and medical students, a mental-health unit for 80 patients and facilities for out-patients. It was commissioned and completed in a record 42 months.

With the exception of the rather heavy canopy designed by the engineers Atelier One, the brick and glass warehouse-look, five-storey front elevation (suggesting wide-span floors reaching from front to back) gives you no indication of what lies behind. The interior design focuses on a naturally ventilated central atrium, rising to seven storeys. It is covered by a pneumatic ETFE (ethylene tetra-fluorothylene) roof membrane. The triple-layer foil membrane forms highly insulated cushions kept inflated by a constant stream of air fed through the extruded aluminium framework. The ground-floor mall creates a semi-outdoor environment, providing seating/café areas, a pharmacy, crèche, hospital chapel and access to all departments in the building via three lift cores. The chapel is an independent structure within the atrium, emphasising the street-like quality of the space. Its stained-glass windows were transferred from the old Westminster Hospital.

Three ante-atria on each side of the central space form light wells at the centre of the wards, and administrative offices run around the perimeter of the building. The walls are lined with horizontal fins called Helmholtz resonators to absorb frequencies of sound which might build up throughout the vast internal spaces. The huge fins at the bottom of each well are part of the natural-ventilation system: open in the summer, they draw cool air in from the outside. Heat generated from the perimeter rooms is used to warm the

Sheppard Robson Architects 1993

atrium in winter. At the rear of the building, housed in a two-storey basement, there is a combined heat and power plant which generates electricity for the hospital; excess power is sold on to the London Electricity Board, feeding into the city's grid. Visual and physical links between all areas of the hospital have been created with uncovered walkways which traverse the central atrium.

The hospital has pioneered an impressive arts programme, with commissioned works by Allen Jones (*Acrobatic Dancer* – see more of Jones' work at the Hilton Hotel, Terminal 4, Heathrow), textiles by Sian Tucker, murals by Melvyn Chantrey, tapestry by Mary Fogg and a hanging by Patrick Heron. To my surprise the building did not have the usual disinfectant/boiled-food aroma that impregnates so many hospitals – 'catering' has wisely been located beyond the rear of the atrium. Before you get that far down the 116-metre-long space your breath has already been taken away by the innumerable innovative features.

ADDRESS Fulham Road, London SW6
CLIENT Riverside Health Authority
CONTRACT VALUE £177 million
SIZE 111,500 square metres
BUS 14, 211 to Fulham Road
ACCESS to the central atrium

Sheppard Robson Architects 1993

MONTEVETRO

The 'glass mountain' is more dry ski slope on this most fragmented of sites on the south side of the river. The luxury development comprises 103 one-, two-, three- and four-bedroom apartments and rooftop penthouses. It has a leisure centre and parking for 170 cars. The site was formerly occupied by Hovis flour mills between 1970s' high-rise housing blocks and the area's outstanding landmark, the Grade I-listed St Mary's church. The diagonal alignment of the building is in direct response to the setting; it creates a new landscaped public park around the church and opens up the river walk as a continuous route between Battersea and Wandsworth bridges.

Five connected blocks rise towards the river from four to 20 storeys. The blocks are connected by four lift towers on the east façade, providing direct access to all flats and avoiding the need for corridors. The concrete frame is clad in terracotta and glass panels with sloping roofs formed from stepped zinc. Balconies are made from structural steelwork suspended from each floor slab.

As a luxury development and with land at a premium, the shape of the building does provide the greatest number of units, all with a river (and Chelsea) view to the west, though the idea was exercised previously at Cascades in Docklands. Had RRP used this model to lead the way in social housing the project might have been more provocative.

ADDRESS confluence of Battersea Church Road, Vicarage Crescent and Battersea High Street, London SW11
CLIENT Taylor Woodrow Capital Developments
CONTRACT VALUE £38 million **SIZE** 23,000 square metres
TUBE none; take a 19 bus to Battersea Bridge Road, then walk
ACCESS none

Richard Rogers Partnership 2000

SHRI SWAMINARAYAN MANDIR, NEASDEN

Caught in the sprawling web of the A404, A406 (commonly known as the North Circular) and A407 is an architectural jewel unlike any other in this guide. The Mandir (the Hindu word for temple) and Haveli (courtyard house – the Cultural Complex) are the first to be built outside the Indian subcontinent. Extensive research was carried out including a study tour of north-west India (where the Aryan people entered India from Persia as early as 5000 BC to form the Vedic civilisation, the precursor of Hinduism). The design process involved close collaboration between the architects, engineers and members of the Swaminarayan Hindu Mission to take account of the British weather and statutory building requirements alongside the wishes of the Mission to have a mandir true to the designs laid down in the ancient architectural texts, the Shilpashastras. However, the existing building is not a replica of any other and its design brought together strands of several ancient architectural styles and methods.

Climate and pollution ruled out the use of red sandstone as the primary building material for the Mandir itself, and Vedic principles ban the use of ferrous materials. Vedic tradition was translated into working drawings to satisfy local authorities and the solution of an inner mandir of marble with a weatherproof outer enclosure of carved limestone was arrived at. The adjacent Haveli – comprising living accommodation for the attendant Sadhus, an administration area and a community meeting place – was developed from the study of the domestic architectural traditions of north-west India. The carved timber (Burmese teak and English oak), adopted from the carved temples of Gujarat, has not been recreated in India or anywhere else in the last 100 years.

The Mandir design incorporates a 7-metre-diameter central mandapa (dome) surrounded by seven conical shikhars (spires) which house the murtis (deities) and provide places beneath for contemplation. Twelve hundred tons of Carrara marble and 3000 tons

WEST AND SOUTH-WEST LONDON

Chandrakant B Sompura/Triad Architects Planners 1995

SHRI SWAMINARAYAN MANDIR, NEASDEN

of Vrataza Bulgarian limestone were shipped tò Kandal in Gujarat where a thousand Indian stonemasons hand-carved the stone before shipping it back to the UK. An additional 920 tons of Ambaji marble were carved in Rajasthan in a specially created workshop near the quarry. Specialist stonemasons and craftsmen were flown to the uk from India to supervise the construction. The intention was to make the structure appear as an organic whole when in fact it was made in finely carved sections.The internal structure is a vast jigsaw-puzzle assembly of marble dowels and light cement.

In India a mandir would be partially open to the elements to provide natural ventilation. In west London underfloor heating and double glazing at ground-floor level are the order of the day, leaving the veil of intricate traceried limestone surrounding the building to convey a sense of airy authenticity. A visit to the Mandir and Haveli is one of the more surprising, profoundly unusual and – yes – truly religious experiences to be had in London. Its appearance on the city's architectural map indicates how building styles and techniques are becoming more global and more adaptable as cultural demands become increasingly specific.

ADDRESS 105/115 Brentfield Road, London NW10
CLIENT Swaminarayan Hindu Mission
STRUCTURAL ENGINEER Austin Trueman
CONTRACT VALUE £25 million
SIZE 10,000 square metres/3.85-hectare site
TUBE Neasden – Jubilee Line
ACCESS open 9.00–12.00 and 16.00–18.00; remove shoes in the foyer area of the Haveli and observe silence in the Mandir

Chandrakant B Sompura/Triad Architects Planners 1995

JUBILEE SCHOOL

There is a renewed interest in examining the use and perception of schools, their effective-ness as patterns of teaching (especially in IT) change, and the role that the buildings and their facilities play in the community. An open competition held in 1997 by Essex Council for a model sustainable primary school was won and subsequently built at Notely Green by AHMM. This set a precedent for the practice in a number of ways, namely a continued rela-tionship with their services engineers to apply principles of shape, orientation and air movement from the single-storey greenfield site in Essex to this two-storey urban location.

This building and its grounds are part of a Lambeth initiative to build four 'new gen-eration' primary schools in the borough. This project amalgamated three schools. In addi-tion to the 420 pupils in the infant and primary school, the building also incorporates a 'SureStart' daycare centre for parents-to-be and young children (SureStart is a govern-ment scheme to help to reduce child poverty and assist in integrating young families into the community by providing training and support) and meets a specific requirement for specialised teaching and support facilities for 30 profoundly deaf children to allow inte-gration into mainstream classes. The school facilities are made available to the wider community throughout the year so certain areas of the building are independently acces-sible out of school hours.

The building is composed of three elements: the hall and administrative block pro-viding a bold street frontage and main entrance; the classroom block with SureStart and nursery facilities; and the Special Educational Needs block with dedicated access at the sheltered rear of the site. The overall architectural statement is dignified in the face of potential fragmentation and separation. An emphasis on horizontality in all of its built ele-ments inscribes a solid and legible ground plane across the sloping site. The position of the building within the large site area maximises views of the sky and school grounds

Allford Hall Monighan Morris (AHMM) 2002

JUBILEE SCHOOL

rather than neighbouring buildings and street activity, providing high-quality natural light to all the classrooms. Chimneys in each classroom are for both light and ventilation.

This is not a quaint or cosy building – it is mildly charismatic, taking on the serious role of a civic building. The International-Style introduction of colour on low rendered walls painted purple and pink and the blue-glazed brick perimeter walls creates a middle ground between the building and its immediate surroundings that bears little relation to either and therefore is of great benefit to both – a device drastically undervalued in the majority of built schemes. The building does not assume childlike forms, wavy lines and mock motifs, and detailing of materials throughout is self-assured rather than obsessive, embodying a flexibility to respond to any future changes.

The design development involved collaborations with graphic designers Studio Myerscough on developing the identities of individual classrooms, artist Martin Richman working as a colourist from the outset of the project in individual classrooms (supported by the Royal Society of Arts). Andrew Stafford developed bespoke furniture, including four types of chair which have the potential for generic reproduction.

WEST AND SOUTH-WEST LONDON

ADDRESS Tulse Hill, London SW2
STRUCTURAL ENGINEER Elliot Wood Partnership
SERVICES ENGINEERS Atelier Ten
SIZE site – approx. 15,000 square metres/school – approximately 4000 square metres
RAIL Tulse Hill
ACCESS restricted

Allford Hall Monighan Morris (AHMM) 2002

KENSINGTON AND CHELSEA

THAMES WATER RING MAIN TOWER

A student competition was held for a structure that would hide a surge pipe in the middle of the Shepherd's Bush roundabout and at the same time celebrate the vast £250 million ring-main project which now embraces central London. The winning entry was designed by students from the Royal College of Art, who created this 15-metre-high barometer. The round tower is made of steel and glass (with the service ladder in the middle) and is animated by coloured water contained within the curved glass walls. This spirals its way up and down the tower to indicate the climatic extremes.

The adjacent classical shed is not related in any way to the winning design and is best ignored.

KENSINGTON AND CHELSEA

ADDRESS Shepherd's Bush roundabout, London W12
CLIENT Thames Water
CONSULTANT ARCHITECT Alan Brooks Associates
STRUCTURAL ENGINEER Neil Thomas
TUBE Shepherd's Bush – Central, Hammersmith & City Lines

Damien O'Sullivan/Tania Doufa 1994

WESTBOURNE GROVE PUBLIC LAVATORIES

The project encompasses the whole of the triangular traffic island to incorporate landscape design as well as the design of the building itself. CZWG's unmistakeable approach comes into its own in this small but provocative urban folly. The three-sided plan has grown out of the shape of the site: the wide end accommodates the lavatories and attendant's kiosk and the pointed end of the triangle is a florist's kiosk. The pale aquamarine glazed-brick walls sit on the pavement like a slice of delectable gateau, topped by a delicate glazed canopy roof with the clock stuck on the corner like a glacé cherry. Each feature is exploited to the full, even down to the stylised supergraphics on the lavatory doors to distinguish the gents from the ladies.

There is no doubt that it is an improvement on its predecessors. It is unusually generous with space when so often minimum standard dimensions are applied for a facility of this type. A bold move by the local residents (the Pembridge Association actually promoted the idea of commissioning CZWG) to change the face of their neighbourhood.

KENSINGTON AND CHELSEA

ADDRESS junction of Colville Road and Westbourne Grove, London W11

CLIENT The Royal Borough of Kensington and Chelsea Council Offices

STRUCTURAL ENGINEER Dewhurst Macfarlane & Partners

CONTRACT VALUE £190,000

SIZE site 700 square metres, building 60 square metres

TUBE Notting Hill Gate – Central, Circle, District Lines/Westbourne Grove – Hammersmith & City Line (both require a 5-minute walk to reach the site)

ACCESS open

CZWG Architects 1993

NATURAL HISTORY MUSEUM

The elaborately decorated Romanesque style of Alfred Waterhouse's museum of 1881 epitomises the Victorian passion for collecting. At the time the building was innovative in its use of cast-iron and steel construction with terracotta tiles. Today the definition of museum as resource and building type is under review with so many collections acquiring new meaning in relation to modern discoveries. In 1988 the neighbouring Geological Museum (1935) was linked to the main building to become the Life Galleries (evolution and ecology), Earth Galleries (volcanoes and earthquakes) and geological collection. So, rather than design new buildings, while some architects at the time were designing shops, others found themselves designing exhibitions. The Ecology Gallery by Ian Ritchie Architects and the Dinosaur Gallery by Herron Associates @ Imagination (both in the Life Galleries) illustrate this approach to museum display and are good examples of how modern interventions can successfully and uncompromisingly converse with the existing dominant structure.

The **ECOLOGY GALLERY** is a chasm of Optiwhite glass, illuminated with coloured lights to create the illusion of fire, water and a sheer glacial wall. Clear strips are cut into walls, like rubbing frost off windows, to reveal exhibits and details of the existing building. Bridges traverse the glass corridor connecting themed exhibits on an upper level. These platforms allow visitors to pause and float in space before being drawn into the walls again to walk inside a leaf or experience being shovelled up by a giant digger.

The **DINOSAUR GALLERY** is a triumph of modernisation and preservation over mundane conservation. An 84-metre raised walkway runs the full length of the gallery. The assembly of steel rods and cables was designed to be held in both tension and compression – a structure that could support itself independently from the existing building. Its function is three-fold. Firstly, the bridge provides new circulation, and new views of the

Ian Ritchie Architects 1991/Herron Associates @ Imagination 1992/HOK 2001

exhibits and details of the existing building. Secondly, it holds all services to illuminate the terracotta carvings of fish and animals which adorn Waterhouse's columns, treading lightly around these parts which were previously out of reach. Thirdly, the structure forms a framework from which to hang dinosaur skeletons (a slight vibration in the cables causes them to twitch ominously).

Both schemes transcend the experience of the traditional museum visit by integrating the journey through the exhibits as part of the process of discovery. The striking contrast between old and new materials and structural propositions casts a flattering light over both past and present.

The latest and largest addition to the museum is phase one of the **DARWIN CENTRE** (HOK International) which houses purpose-designed laboratories for 100 scientists and creates a home for more than 22 million zoological specimens (known as the Spirit Collection). The building embodies the museum's new approach to opening up the collections to the public, an attempt to increase understanding of the research work carried out behind the scenes. The design of the building affects this notion of transparency and adopts zoomorphic imagery and behavioral patterns within its built fabric. It comprises three sections: in the front are offices and laboratories placed behind a glass façade; at the back is an eight-storey cold store for the specimens; and separating the two is an atrium for public access. The triple-skin glass façade (engineered by Arup Façade Engineering) is held in place by claw-like brackets and sun-tracking metal louvers (with built-in electric sensors) change across its surface in a reptilian manner, drawing air up from ground level and out through a linear chimney at the top to provide an efficient cooling system. The curved, undulating roof is made of very lightweight inflated cushions (devised by Vector Special Systems, who previously implemented this material at the

Ian Ritchie Architects 1991/Herron Associates @ Imagination 1992/HOK 2001

NATURAL HISTORY MUSEUM

Chelsea and Westminster Hospital; see pages 24–26) clamped between yellow steel ribs. The cushions are made from a recyclable plastic called ethyltetrafluoroethylene (ETFE) that is self-cleaning, anti-static, is transparent to UV light and possesses thermal properties that are equal to triple glazing. The atrium is bisected by occupied bridges exposing the activities between store and laboratory.

The building is academic in its interpretation of its function (it looks like a building for research). It incorporates 'responsive' and 'intelligent' building elements into conventional walls, floors and ceilings rather than challenging the built form as a whole and in this sense it also serves as a building that is itself a research project.

Phase two (due for completion in 2007) will replace the old 1920s Spirit Building which will in turn open up views of the phase one building from Cromwell Road.

KENSINGTON AND CHELSEA

ADDRESS Cromwell Road, London SW7
CLIENT Natural History Museum
TUBE South Kensington – Circle, District, Piccadilly Lines
ACCESS open daily, 10.00–17.50

Ian Ritchie Architects 1991/Herron Associates @ Imagination 1992/HOK 2001

SCIENCE MUSEUM: RECENT ADDITIONS

The Museum of Ornamental Art opened in 1852 and subsequently grew to become what is now the Science Museum. By definition this institution continues a process of updating and re-presenting of a constantly growing collection that now comprises more than 300,000 objects. Only 10 per cent of the collection is actually on display in the museum, from Stephenson's Rocket locomotive of 1829 to an obese mouse, genetically engineered in 1999. The original building was designed by Sir Richard Allison in 1913. He used the department store as the model for the inside for generous circulation and the Edwardian office building for the exterior. Over the years the building has been expanded to accommodate new acquisitions and displays. More recently this includes The Basement by Ben Kelly Design (BKD, 1995), The Challenge of Materials Gallery by Chris Wilkinson Architects (1998) and The Wellcome Wing by MacCormac Jamieson Prichard (2000).

THE BASEMENT is specifically designed for the museum's younger visitors and school parties combining exhibits in playroom/galleries with a large communal picnic area called the Terrace (much like a gently raked football terrace). It was a unique opportunity for the designers to de-institutionalise an institution and devise a plan that would open a child's mind to the wonders of science. The Arcade runs the full length of the space behind the Terrace to provide unhindered disabled access to the entire plan (instead of confining all disabled visitors to designated zones, as in so many public facilities – see Tate Modern, page 120–124). Key to the project's success is BKD's ability to integrate strong colour, durable yet tactile materials and a sense of humour into all the facilities. Every element from floor surfaces (designed in collaboration with artist Tim Head) to the colour-coded sections of the building's structure that have been cut away to form the present interior space, have been considered as a way of engaging a child in a given activity. This is an exercise not in dumbing-down but in switching-on.

various architects 1995/1998/2000

SCIENCE MUSEUM: RECENT ADDITIONS

THE CHALLENGE OF MATERIALS GALLERY reinstates the two-storey atrium (previously closed off) of the first main gallery encountered by visitors on their arrival. New displays have been created on the mezzanine spaces connected at first-floor level by the centrepiece of the project – an elegant 12-metre-long suspension bridge. The purpose of the bridge is to inform visitors about modern materials, using interactive means. The floor is made of laminated-glass sections, suspended by four cobwebs of stainless-steel wires, each measuring less than 1 millimetre in diameter. Like their natural counterparts, these disappear under certain lighting conditions. The wires are attached to stress gauges connected to a fibre-optic display and synthesiser, so as you cross the bridge sound effects (provided by Ron Geesin) and light conditions change according to the variation in load.

THE WELLCOME WING is the latest and largest (at 11,000 square metres) addition to the Science Museum. The wing accommodates exhibition space, circulation, an IMAX cinema and restaurant and is the climax to the museum's new chronological exhibition, 'The Making of the Modern World'. The building is conceived as a single volume within which are suspended three levels of adaptable floor space projecting off the 30-metre-x-30-metre double-glazed blue back wall, with the IMAX cinema hanging overhead off the party wall between old and new buildings. The main structure is of concrete columns with horizontal steel trusses supported by large pivoted steel 'gerberettes'. The gerberettes shorten the span of the trusses and so substantially reduce their depth and weight. The load is transferred to the foundations by vertical tie rods. The gerberettes also detach the exhibition floors and IMAX walls from the main shell so that they appear to be suspended in space. The theme of lightness, translucency and transparency is continued throughout; all walls are suffused with blue light and layered with projection screens, and floor surfaces such as fine steel grill change their density according to obliqueness of view. The

KENSINGTON AND CHELSEA

various architects 1995/1998/2000

blue wall was a collaborative work designed by architect, structural and service engineers, glass manufacturers Schott-Desag and lighting designers Hollands Licht. It is a three-layered construction of glass and fixed louvres designed to achieve a fine balance between daylight and internal lighting. The architect's choice of colour was inspired by 'the deep blue of Yves Klein and a sense of depth of field by a James Turrell installation. Both are evocative of the highly electronic age in which we live'. Meanwhile, a banal level of interactivity and graphic overdose smother the exhibition displays. So, stirring in its blueness it may be – but equipped for new ways of looking at scientific information, it appears doubtful. As so many of the exhibits on display throughout the museum show, there is nothing more evocative than discovery itself.

KENSINGTON AND CHELSEA

ADDRESS Exhibition Road, London SW7
CLIENT Science Museum
TUBE South Kensington – Circle, District, Piccadilly Lines
ACCESS open daily, 10.00–17.50

various architects 1995/1998/2000

SERPENTINE GALLERY

Designed by J Grey West on a symmetrical Palladian plan as the Serpentine Tea Pavilion (1934), the building has been a public gallery since 1970. More recently, lottery funding has made possible extensive changes in order to provide adequate storage and security, temperature and humidity control and a watertight roof.

As the building is Grade II-listed and owned by the Royal Parks, any visible additions had to be in character with the existing fabric. External repairs were carried out using Westmoreland slate and bricks from the original supplier. Structurally, the most significant change is the excavation of a basement to house a plant room, stores and a workshop. A concrete slab was cast on the ground floor and then dug out from beneath.

The gallery spaces have been maintained in profile but the route has been formalised. However, the quality of the spaces has been altered by the introduction of skylights with external automatic sunscreen blinds, a new internal artificial-lighting system, air-conditioning, security shutters embedded in the ceilings and a continuous surface of granolithic tiles on the floor.

Formerly visitors could wander casually from the park into the gallery through tall French doors on the north and east sides. Now the entrance has been consolidated with the bookshop, lavatories and foyer. Landscaping of the area surrounding the gallery was executed in close collaboration with the Royal Parks landscape architect Hal Moggridge. The forecourt incorporates the first permanent Ian Hamilton Finlay installation in London.

ADDRESS Kensington Gardens, Hyde Park, London W2
STRUCTURAL ENGINEER WSP Consulting Engineers
TUBE South Kensington – Circle, District, Piccadilly Lines
ACCESS open daily, 10.00–18.00

KENSINGTON AND CHELSEA

John Miller & Partners 1997

THE MONSOON BUILDING

Formerly the Paddington Maintenance Depot, this building has marked the journey between east and west London over the triumphant A40 Westway since it was designed by Bicknell & Hamilton in 1969. In the early 1990s, having been derelict for years, it was Grade II listed. Its unmistakeable presence, part-factory, part-ship, part-modernist villa, was undiminished during this period: it became the site of illegal parties and the spiritual home of the cyber-punk band Mutoid Waste.

179 Harrow Road has been cleaned up; concrete frame scrubbed, cream mosaic skin restored, double-glazed units installed. The interior has been resuscitated as open-plan office space for Monsoon with a staff restaurant on the fourth floor on a level with the elevated road. Now that rooms are cooled and heated by chilled beams in the ceilings the redundant plant room makes for exotic office space with the most senior management (the captains of this industry) claiming the top floor 'bridge' and roof terrace. A triple-height void has been inserted into the reception area opening up views through the interior. The east end is defined by the original top lit lozenge-shaped staircase, coated in turquoise mosaic tiles and expressed externally by the double funnels at the prow of the building.

The neighbouring Oval Building (a former vehicle depot) has been refurbished to shell status. Improved pedestrian access is an integral part of the scheme with links to and across the Regent's Canal and the development at Paddington Basin.

ADDRESS 179 Harrow Road, London W2
CLIENTS Monsoon Accessorize Ltd and Wymore Ltd – The Peter Simon Family Fund
STRUCTURAL ENGINEER Price & Myers **SERVICES ENGINEER** Atelier Ten
TUBE Paddington – Bakerloo, Hammersmith & City, Circle, District Lines
ACCESS restricted

Allford Hall Monaghan Morris 2001

PADDINGTON BASIN

Paddington Basin, currently under construction, is just part of an even bigger plan that extends west along the canal to encompass the development at Paddington Central, together forming the largest designated regeneration area in central London. The two most important aspects of this site are its location, adjacent to Paddington Station and the Heathrow Express connecting central London with its largest international airport in 15 minutes, and its proximity to St Mary's hospital campus. The masterplan for the Basin area around the canal wharf includes a mix of commercial, leisure and residential usage and the creation of a major recreational resource for this part of London.

Four key developments dominate the site: The Point, Waterside, The Windings and The Grand Union Building. Each of these buildings is designed to create a robust architectural form and identity for the site. **THE POINT**, due to house the UK headquarters of Orange, with its tug-boat-shaped plan and ten storeys, is not the clunky postmodern Farrell we recognise from Vauxhall (page 104) or the Embankment but is altogether sleeker and quieter in its execution. It clearly makes the distinction between this architect's personal oeuvre in the design of single buildings and the practice's increasing reputation in the field of urban planning and design. The building has two main entrances to accommodate different tenancy options with a central bank of lifts. Elevations incorporate full-height glazing. The ground-floor is set behind a colonnade of concrete columns. Levels 1–6 are articulated by vertical metal fins that in turn provide a framework for timber brise-soleils on the south side. On the north side the fins hold a light shelf that reflects light into the offices. The top three floors are wrapped in a smooth glazed skin.

WATERSIDE (the yellow steelwork is the first indication that this is a building by RRP) will soon be the headquarters of Marks & Spencer. It comprises two connected 13-storey blocks, cut back to form triangular plans that will include contained external

masterplan Terry Farrell Partnership 2003

spaces facing on to the canal. Following the RRP method of placing the services on the outside, the building itself comprises 'served space', the main occupied floorplates have services and circulation towers at each corner.

THE WINDINGS by Jestico & Whiles, separating the two RRP schemes, will be a nine-storey block of approximately 200 homes. At the time of writing this scheme had outline planning approval and will begin on site in mid 2003.

Its immediate neighbour will be RRP's **GRAND UNION BUILDING**, a cluster of three tiered blocks, the tallest reaching 31 storeys. The two taller blocks are for commercial use, the smaller of the three is for residential purposes, offering 291 homes of which 115 units are designated as affordable housing (30 for social rented housing, 29 for low-cost shared ownership and 56 homes for key workers). The office buildings provide maximum flexibility for future letting strategies. The floor plates are conceived in sets, either as six separate offices across any given floor or as a group set linked via an atrium to create one large floorplate. The building envelopes comprise solar shading contained within a climate-moderating triple-glazed wall system. A combination of mechanical and low-energy cooling systems such as chilled ceilings and beams regulate themselves automatically and according to the occupancy of the building.

A strategy for landscaping the area has been developed by landscape architects, Gillespies. Their idea is to incorporate landscape into building plans and then extend the public space around the base of the buildings to connect to the surrounding amenities. A series of three innovative glass bridges is proposed to span the wharf. These will be designed by artists and designers – Langlands & Bell, Marcus Taylor and Thomas Heatherwick's Studio. Eighty mooring posts for barges are to be managed by British Waterways, 20 of which will provide retail and commercial premises for local businesses.

masterplan Terry Farrell Partnership 2003

PADDINGTON BASIN

As with all large areas of regeneration, it will be interesting to see how the proposition will take hold of the site over time and influence existing buildings and services in the area. At present North Wharf Road is also home to a beleaguered set of Portakabins that serve as a school. Developers have been pressurised by London's mayor, Ken Livingstone, into granting a limited amount of space for affordable housing. Now both parties must ensure genuine long-term stability and well-being for the area by investing in fundamentally essential amenities such as schools and nurseries.

KENSINGTON AND CHELSEA

ADDRESS North Wharf Road, London
CLIENT Paddington Basin Developments Ltd, a joint venture between Chelsfield plc and European Land and Property
TUBE Paddington – Bakerloo, Hammersmith & City, Circle, District Lines
ACCESS restricted to individual buildings but public areas are open

masterplan Terry Farrell Partnership 2003

WESTMINSTER

PORTCULLIS HOUSE

Portcullis House appears only to occupy the corner site of Bridge Street and Victoria Embankment. However, the architect's scheme notionally extends the perimeter of the building to Richmond Terrace, Parliament Street, and below ground to Westminster Underground Station. The design of the parliamentary building and the underground station has been closely integrated, the substructure of the station (the only part actually open to the public) providing structural support for the building. Portcullis House provides 200 offices for members of parliament and their staff. These are arranged over seven floors around a central courtyard which brings daylight into all the office spaces above ground level. The idea was to create a parliamentary 'campus' made up of a network of collegiate spaces using courtyards and alleys rather than tunnels or bridges to connect old (the Victorian and Edwardian buildings of Richard Norman Shaw) and new buildings. Portcullis House has been designed to last 200 years as opposed to the average new building's 30 years.

Public areas, such as the Select Committee Rooms and conference and dining rooms, are located on the river side of the building to orientate the building with the Palace of Westminster. The glass-covered courtyard (descendant of the atrium of the 1980s – see also The Great Court on pages 176–178) provides a semi-outdoor environment equipped with tree-lined cafés, presumably an attempt to make MPs forget that they are in a bullet-proof compound. The courtyard roof structure, a lavish mixture of glass and timber resting on low stone arches, starts out as Buckminster Fuller geodesic envelope and finishes up as neo-medieval vaulted ceiling – an unlikely sequence.

The building prides itself on its integrated design/environmental criteria: the external Derbyshire gritstone piers diminish in width, carrying less weight as they rise, balanced by widening bronze air ducts to either side. These ducts carry stale air up and

Michael Hopkins & Partners 2000

across the roof line to be pumped out through the 14 blackened bronze chimney stacks. The rooms are cooled by water from a 140-metre-deep borehole which is then poured back into the Thames. Inside, the absence of painted surfaces is refreshing. All walls are either of polished concrete or fitted with pale oak cupboards and shelves. The gently curved ceilings for directing natural light are a Hopkins' trademark.

On completion this building was voted the nation's ugliest, although some sought to defend it in terms of quality and its deliberate avoidance of fashion. But I am suspicious of a building that denies the people access to what should be a strictly public space; costs so much to build; has all the pretensions of a modern use of traditional English building skills yet holds so much metaphor; and erects a Dickensian image of London to house modern government.

It is interesting to note that among several investigations into how areas of the budget were allocated in the building, the Harman Report (Harman being a cladding contractor) called into question the way that 'best value' is assessed. The company successfully sued the House of Commons for picking a more expensive UK rival for the contract to clad Portcullis House. The client has to explain to the bidders exactly how any test will be applied before they tender. If this is not explained then the only lawful criterion is lowest price.

ADDRESS corner of Bridge Street and Victoria Embankment, London SW1
STRUCTURAL AND SERVICES ENGINEER Ove Arup & Partners
CONTRACT VALUE £250 million
TUBE Westminster – Jubilee Line
ACCESS restricted

Michael Hopkins & Partners 2000

CHANNEL 4 HEADQUARTERS

This is a key modern building in the heart of Westminster. The territory is stalked by the colossal Department of the Environment blocks waiting on Death Row, the corpse of what was Westminster Hospital, the charmless DSS office just down the road and the Royal Horticultural Society buildings (1904 and 1928). Not exactly showbiz. Channel 4's building, comprising an underground car park, TV studios and offices, a development of 100 apartments (by Lyons Sleeman + Hoare) and a garden square, has made a considerable impact on its business and residential neighbours by introducing a lively industry to the area.

There are four blocks around a central garden. The north and west sides are occupied by Channel 4, the south and east sides are residential. The L-shaped office area butts up to the street but a generous recess into the corner has been given over to a dramatic entrance. The approach is across a bridge over what appears to be a glass pool, but is actually the roof of an underground studio. To your left is a stack of boxes (conference rooms) held in an elegant framework of tapered beams; to the right external lifts cling to a service tower and transmission antennae. The entrance itself is through a concave glass curtain – which appears to be hung from a row of curtain claws – draped between the two wings to allow a glimpse of the reception, restaurant and garden beyond.

The contrast between the parts of the building is what makes it so distinctive, but the elements also work together to form a varied, relatively low-level landscape. Each part seems to have a clear agenda, and the entrance holds no bars.

WESTMINSTER

ADDRESS Horseferry Road, London SW1
STRUCTURAL ENGINEER Ove Arup & Partners
TUBE St James' Park – Circle, District Lines
ACCESS restricted

Richard Rogers Partnership 1991–94

BUCKINGHAM PALACE TICKET OFFICE

Buckingham Palace has started to open its doors to visitors during August and September each year. The brief for a ticket office called for a demountable, storable structure which could be used for five years. The prefabricated timber office cabin is brought to the site in two parts (mounted on wheels) and bolted together. Birch-faced plywood ribs are bolted to the steel chassis to make the frame and then the whole is clad externally with Western red-cedar strips and sealed with yacht varnish. It is surrounded by a timber deck which floats on adjustable feet to conceal the wheels of the cabin once it is in position.

A tensile-fabric canopy covers the area defined by the edges of the deck. It is supported on two elliptical Glulam timber masts (one at either end of the cabin) with a main keel beam running between them. The beam is bolted to the cabin with steel plates which slice into the laminated-timber edge above the teller windows. A series of struts attached to the main beam extends outwards horizontally, tied by vertical tensile cables to concrete blocks in the ground.

This is a building which fits the season and its setting. It uses a vocabulary of details derived from marquees, boats and elegant travelling cases – the cabin alone is like the portmanteau I imagine Her Majesty might take on holiday.

WESTMINSTER

ADDRESS Lower Grosvenor Place, London SW1
STRUCTURAL ENGINEER Ove Arup & Partners
TUBE Green Park – Piccadilly, Victoria Lines, then walk across the park to the Canada Gate entrance
ACCESS open in August and September only

Michael Hopkins & Partners 1994

SACKLER GALLERIES
ROYAL ACADEMY OF ARTS

Norman Foster joins a short but distinguished list of architects who have contributed to the Royal Academy's evolution. Burlington House was built in 1666. The front elevation was remodelled by Colen Campbell from 1717 to 1720, with a garden façade by Samuel Ware added in 1815 and an extension by Sidney Smirke in 1867. A gap, almost 5 metres wide, between the garden façade and this extension is the site for Foster's contribution, which provides circulation up to the previously isolated third-storey Diploma Galleries.

From the atmosphere of a narrow Victorian alley at ground level, visitors are rapidly transported by a glass-walled, hydraulic lift through three floors past the renovated exteriors of Smirke and Ware. At the top you are dazzled by bright white light through translucent glass all around, and the vast, sculpted head of a Greek god resting on the parapet of Smirke's façade creates a bizarre and dramatic sense of scale and great distance.

At the end, across a delicate glass bridge, is a cool, open ante-room where you can sit and view Michelangelo's *Virgin and Child with Infant St John*, and catch another look back along the sculpture gallery. This series of spaces, which floats structurally independent between the old buildings, is simply defined by light and subtle changes in materials. Glazed edges around the floor surfaces help to make the distinction between the old and new techniques. The three Diploma Galleries (now the Sackler Galleries) were gutted, their flat roofs demolished and two barrel-vaulted ceilings with roof lights installed.

WESTMINSTER

ADDRESS Piccadilly, London W1
STRUCTURAL ENGINEER YRM Anthony Hunt Associates
HISTORIC BUILDINGS CONSULTANT Julian Harrap Associates
TUBE Piccadilly Circus – Bakerloo, Piccadilly Lines; Green Park – Piccadilly, Victoria Lines
ACCESS open daily, 10.00–17.30

Foster Associates 1989–91

WALLACE COLLECTION

The Wallace Collection was started by the first Marquess of Hertford in the eighteenth century, handed down and added to by three subsequent generations and finally inherited by the fourth marquess's illegitimate son, Sir Richard Wallace (died 1890). Hertford House was built in 1779 by the fourth Duke of Manchester to take advantage of the duck shooting nearby and bought by the second marquess 20 years later. The collection has been housed here since 1897 and opened to the public in 1900.

The role and perception of a collection today is quite different to that of three centuries ago. Many objects have aged and require cleaning or restoration – through this much can be learned about the way they were made. There is an increasing desire to appreciate the spatial qualities of the buildings housing collections, and no doubt to make them pay. Therefore, the brief here included expansion of the galleries, improvement of educational facilities and creation of a café.

The inner courtyard and the museum vaults were excavated to house the reserve collection, education facility, lecture theatre, two additional galleries, archives and library – all below ground. The café is located in the new ground-floor sculpture court. Symmetrical stone steps with glass balustrading link the levels on either side of the café entrance. The whole courtyard space is enclosed by a lightweight glass-roofed canopy.

The bland café is an unfortunate focus for these latest developments – no doubt quite deliberately, it's rather ladies-who-lunch. A visit to the Wallace Collection is still one of those rare central London surprises.

WESTMINSTER

ADDRESS Hertford House, Manchester Square, London W1
TUBE Bond Street – Central and Jubilee Lines
ACCESS open Monday to Saturday, 10.00–17.00; Sunday,12.00–17.00

Rick Mather Architects 2000

SANDERSON HOTEL

Built in 1958 and designed by Jeff Holyrood of Slater and Uren, this was the headquarters of Sanderson, a furnishing-fabric company. The structure, technologically advanced for its time, could accommodate changes of internal layout and use. The building was planned around an open, inner courtyard with a Japanese garden designed by Phillip Hicks, an original glass mural by John Piper and mosaics by Jupp Dernbach-Mayern. It became Grade II-listed in 1991.

Ian Shrager established his reputation in the 1980s with architect Phillipe Stark by his side, pioneering the 'boutique hotel' in the US. The relatively cheap chic of the Paramount and Royalton in New York defined a new era for hotels that responded to contemporary movie-star and magazine culture. Travellers were getting younger and their budgets bigger – Schrager offered an alternative to the characterless Hilton or the traditional Algonquin.

This, the second Schrager hotel to open in London (its just-about-older sister is in St Martin's Lane), bears all the hallmarks of the team albeit they are taking on London some 15 years after their work in New York. Described as an 'Urban Spa' – the Sanderson is essentially an unbridled display of 'opulence, glamour and style as well as spirituality and well-being with a healthy dose of wit and restraint'. It is the stuff of fantasies where Louis XIV-style furniture sits next to that of Salvador Dali, antique chairs from Tanzania, Eero Aarnio's 'Hanging Bubble' chair and work by various European video artists.

In reality it means a 150-room hotel centred around the inner courtyard and indoor/outdoor lobby. In line with the flexible intentions of the original plans, the only solid walls are perceived to be those of the exterior – internal space is divided by floor-to-ceiling curtains creating flowing and ethereal space; bathrooms in the guestrooms are glass boxes draped in layers of silk. The provision of an additional layer of cotton wool for

Phillipe Stark 2000

SANDERSON HOTEL

guests takes the form of the Agua Bathhouse – health and beauty treatments in an environment that makes you feel like you have died and gone to heaven (although I never thought it would be this tacky).

Spoon+ at Sanderson offers the original 'mix-and-match' menu as orchestrated by Alain Ducasse. This DIY culinary concept comprises low-cholesterol, low-fat and no-carbohydrate ingredients – more of a shadow of the food itself, much like the diners. If you require something with a little more bulk, a cocktail served at either the Purple Bar or the 31-metre Long Bar could provide more sustenance.

WESTMINSTER

ADDRESS 50 Berners Street, London W1
CLIENT Ian Shrager London Ltd
TUBE Oxford Circus – Central, Victoria and Bakerloo lines
ACCESS open – check-in time 15.00; check-out time 12.00

Phillipe Stark 2000

ROYAL OPERA HOUSE COVENT GARDEN

The architect was appointed in 1984 to design a strategy, rather than a scheme, to modernise the Royal Opera House and all its supporting activities in what is a city quarter rather than a single building. The brief required that the front and back of house be addressed, and the issue of integrating the place as a whole into the fabric of London. Although the content has changed radically the continuity of design has remained.

The original opera house building was designed by E M Barry in 1858 to replace a theatre designed by Robert Smirke (see The Great Court at the British Museum, pages 176–178) in 1809 that burned down. A grand extension programme was initiated in the 1980s to meet commercial demands, that is, increasing office and retail space. Westminster Council approved the extension proposals although the Covent Garden Community Association had attempted to intervene by insisting that the ROH site be dedicated to cultural uses. However, by 1989 director Jeremy Isaacs saw it as vital to increase the arts space in order to maintain and advance the Opera House as a useful and internationally competitive facility, so the scheme was revised. By the time this draft was presented in 1994 the National Lottery had been launched and after a rigorous review of the office element of the scheme (which was dropped entirely) the third scheme was granted permission in 1995. This was essentially the scheme as built.

Barry's original auditorium is Grade-I listed and has been refurbished. Interventions have been made to improve sightlines, acoustics, audience comfort, access, facilities, capacity and lighting while the essence of the original space and detailing remains. The stalls have been re-raked, re-aligned and the amphitheatre extended. Materials have been adjusted to reduce sound absorbency. Environmental control has been modernised.

Public access is key to the project so the delay (from 1993 to 1995) had its advantages in allowing certain aspects of the scheme to be developed. The Floral Hall evolved

Dixon Jones BDP 1984–2000

into a public space, main foyer and focus for the project with its escalator link to the amphitheatre level and open-air loggia overlooking the piazza for interval strolls. This new link enabled hierarchical access to the auditorium to be eliminated – now everyone enters through the porte-cochère and foyers rather than separate side stairs. The original Floral Hall was eight bays long but four were given over to stage space, so a mirror is employed to recreate the effect. Its roof is a copy of the lost original. The Studio Theatre (an orchestral rehearsal space catering for chamber opera, dance and educational events for an audience of 400) was also added to the project at this point. Backstage, the new scheme provides space to construct and retain sets for six productions at any one time. These can be moved on automatic stage wagons in an unobstructed three-storey volume between Russell and Floral Streets. Workspaces (for anything from wig-making to dressing rooms) accommodating up to 1000 people are all on top-floor levels with views and natural lighting where possible enhancing the notion of 'a city within a city'.

The pedestrian mid-block connection between Bow Street and Covent Garden piazza (originally designed by Inigo Jones) is fundamental to the request that the ROH be connected to neighbouring streets. By employing arcades (taking their cue from a nineteenth-century arcade on the site) the architects have created ambiguous space which can belong to both building and street. Shops have been integrated wherever possible on the ground level to activate Covent Garden life. The architect states that they were 'interested in the composite expression normally found in a large urban block. Rather than looking for consistency, we worked in various styles simultaneously, creating a collage – a historic neo-classical style on the square; modern street façades and repair and reconstruction to existing nineteenth-century façades elsewhere'. The project is a series of separate buildings with stone used as the common façade material. The classical street

ROYAL OPERA HOUSE COVENT GARDEN

elevations remain almost unchanged. For the modern façades the stone is thin and two-dimensional compared with the traditional use of stone as a carved material. The roof area is treated similarly as a collection of ROH activities and terraces with an enlarged fly-tower clad in Victorian dress rising out of the busy mass. Critic Kenneth Powell politely describes the elevations as 'a progressive development of strict historicism'.

Regardless of the facial expression spread across the collection of buildings, which aims to please everyone and as a result satisfies no-one, the merits of the scheme are clear. The importance of maintaining such a facility in an area saturated by commercialism, and in a way that encourages people (whether they are going to a performance or not) to access the buildings in many ways, can only contribute to the diversity of the city.

ADDRESS Bow Street, London WC2
CLIENT Royal Opera House
STRUCTURAL AND SERVICES ENGINEER Ove Arup & Partners
CONTRACT VALUE £140 million
SIZE 6100 square metres
TUBE Covent Garden – Piccadilly Line
ACCESS public areas open, interiors during performances. Telephone 020 7304 4000 for information

Dixon Jones BDP 1984–2000

SAINSBURY WING
NATIONAL GALLERY

The site was acquired by HM Government in 1959. Lack of funds prevented development until 1980 when the then Secretary of State, Michael Heseltine, proposed a competition to develop the site commercially with galleries on the upper floors. Ahrends Burton & Koralek were chosen to produce designs. In 1984 the Prince of Wales famously denounced abk's scheme as 'a monstrous carbuncle on the face of a much-loved and elegant friend': not surprisingly, planning permission was refused. The present scheme was conceived early in 1985. The Sainsbury brothers offered to fund the extension and in January 1986 Venturi, Scott Brown's designs were selected. The Prince laid the foundation stone.

The aesthetics of the building (a steel and concrete frame clad in the same Portland stone as the original building designed by William Wilkins in 1838) derive from Venturi's postmodern theories, reinterpreting the past and placing it in the present. All of Wilkins' classical elements have been reproduced and then dissected. Inside, the grand stairway in charcoal-black granite has a stately presence while the vast, arched steel trusses above, mimicking the parts of a coarse Victorian train shed, are just some of the many incongruities that lurk in the building.

Venturi's own words sum up the building and his attitude to his architecture: 'It is very sophisticated. You have to be "cultured" to like it.' How many of those whom he calls 'the relatively unsophisticated people' who visit the gallery are prepared to swallow that?

ADDRESS Trafalgar Square, London SW1
ASSOCIATED UK ARCHITECT Sheppard Robson Architects
TUBE Charing Cross – Bakerloo, Jubilee, Northern Lines
ACCESS open Monday to Saturday, 10.00–18.00; Sunday, 14.00–18.00. Closed on bank holidays

WESTMINSTER

Venturi, Scott Brown & Associates, Inc. 1988–91

HUNGERFORD BRIDGE

In 1845 Isambard Kingdom Brunel built a suspension footbridge to serve Hungerford fruit and vegetable market. The market tried to resist competition from nearby Covent Garden by adding a floor for meat and fish and then another to accommodate an art gallery – in vain, the entire premises burnt down in 1854. Coincidentally, the site was immediately cleared to make way for Charing Cross station. Brunel's bridge was replaced by the present railway bridge, designed by Sir John Hawshaw in 1864.

The grim footbridge that was later incorporated into Hawshaw's bridge has at last been addressed. Hungerford Bridge is the key link between the centre of the city and the south side of the river. Lifschutz Davidson's scheme attaches a new footbridge to either side of the railway bridge, to gain unobstructed views up and down stream. The original design for the footbridges showed two 315-metre-long and 4-metre-wide suspension structures with an additional footbridge between Brunel's original brick Surrey Pier and the South Bank. However, while drilling to make the foundation piles in the water a number of unexploded WW2 bombs were discovered. It was decided to move the foundations on to the land which, with the resulting costs, significantly altered the original design. However, the essential idea – that of cantilevered decks hung from inclined pylons – has remained intact. The web of cabling employed and the sheer size of the pylons appear to defy gravity, only adding to the great visual weight of the original railway bridge. Both bridges are now open and are better used than viewed.

ADDRESS connects The Embankment with the South Bank
ENGINEER WSP Group
TUBE Embankment – District and Circle Lines
ACCESS open

WESTMINSTER

Lifschutz Davidson 2002

HAMPDEN GURNEY SCHOOL

The brief was to replace a 1950s school with a six-storey primary school for 240 pupils and 52 homes located in the old playground (the latter due for completion in 2003). Profits from the sale of the flats fund construction of the school. The challenge for the architects was one of density: how to incorporate enough play area in a smaller footprint. The solution has been to create a covered play area on each storey overlooking the street, linked by bridge across a light well to the classrooms at the rear. A nursery occupies the ground floor – children move up the building as they get older. Administration areas, library, multimedia room, hall, chapel and drama rooms occupy the lower-ground-floor level.

A steel frame with an arched truss at roof level carries the centre structure in tension, enabling the school hall at lower ground level to be column-free. A tensile roof creates a large column-free group teaching room or 'technology garden' on the roof. The elevations are defined by the 1.9-metre glass balustrading at each level allowing the playgrounds (or 'playdecks') to hover in the air and children to engage safely in the activities of the street. The strategy readdresses the harsh landscaping (so brutal to so many knees) associated with traditional school playgrounds. The vertical hierarchy that has been set up from necessity is not unlike the arrangement found in the many Edwardian school buildings around the city. What is different is the lack of any collective playground area which does puts an onus on the school body to invent new activities that include pupils of all ages.

ADDRESS Nutford Place, London W1
CLIENTS Hampden Gurney School Trustees and Jarvis Construction
STRUCTURAL ENGINEER BDP **M&S ENGINEER** Excelsior Services
TUBE Marble Arch – Central Line
ACCESS restricted

BDP 2002

SOUTH LONDON

CITY HALL
GREATER LONDON AUTHORITY HEADQUARTERS

This is the home of the new London Assembly and its chamber, the offices of the Mayor of London and 500 staff of the Greater London Authority (GLA). They represent the return of a form of government absent since the abolition of the Greater London Council in 1986. The Mayor's main role is 'to develop London-wide strategies ... for major public services ... embracing police, transport, fire and emergency planning, regeneration, planning, sustainability and environmental issues, cultural affairs, health concerns ... and the general promotion of London'. The Assembly meets in public (see www.london.gov.uk for details) to examine the Mayor's activities and investigate issues of importance to Londoners, to publish its findings and make recommendations to the Mayor. The GLA is not a traditional local authority but 'exists to provide strategic direction for the future of London'.

Equipped with this political model, a symbolic architectural one was developed around similar buzz words: 'democracy, accessibility and sustainability' – essentially a public building and space for the citizens of London. The surrounding 5.5-hectares are the subject of a larger masterplan, also devised by Foster & Partners and currently under phased construction. Most notable at present are the terrific views that have opened up across the river and the lack of cars. But 'streetscape', that most ominous word, is used in publicity material to describe a future provision of 'amenities including shops, restaurants and cafés ... and five large office buildings'. No mention of how a masterplan might meet the neighbourhood skirting the development area with its run-down council housing, neglected churchyards and railway arches rich in light industry.

Which brings us to that shape: an egg, a crash helmet, a glass testicle, the last accompanied by its dismembered appendage across the river, the 40-storey Swiss Re tower – 'the erotic gherkin' – graceless images conjured up by journalists. The form of City Hall is defined by a half-kilometre-long ramp that spirals through all of its ten storeys. The

Foster and Partners 2002

CITY HALL

citizen's journey begins in a café and room displaying a strangely truncated model of central London in the basement, moving up to the assembly chamber on the second floor and a viewing gallery with views through a triangulated glass façade towards the Tower of London. Further up the ramp are views in to the GLA offices and more panoramic scenes of the city surmounted by an exhibition/function room called the 'London Living Room'.

The building's form contains the greatest volume with the least surface area exposed to direct sunlight. Its stepped floorplates provide shading for offices beneath. Perimeter offices are naturally ventilated by manually operated vents beneath the windows and cold groundwater is pumped via boreholes into chilled beams in the ceilings. It is estimated that the annual energy consumption for the building's mechanical systems will be approximately one quarter that of a typical air-conditioned office.

And yet for all these worthy credentials, the computer-modelling techniques employed to achieve its geometry and the high-tech lasers used to cut the glazing panels (each one unique), there is no harmony in the execution. There is no detail. Anyone who has walked down the ramp inside Frank Lloyd Wright's Guggenheim Museum in New York (designed in 1943 and built in 1956–59) will have enjoyed the clarity of the gesture there. Here, there is a sense of a desperate need to seize and take hold of the site by any means necessary. It must be seen as a work-in-progress, and not as great work.

ADDRESS The Queen's Walk, London SE1
CLIENT CIT Group Ltd
STRUCTURAL ENGINEER Arup
TUBE London Bridge – Northern Line/Tower Hill – Circle, District lines
ACCESS weekdays only, 8.00–20.00

SOUTH LONDON

Foster and Partners 2002

VAUXHALL CROSS

Vauxhall Cross is MI6's headquarters. Until they moved here, the secret services had been housed inconspicuously in indistinguishable 1960s office buildings around London. A new image is being nurtured.

This is a bespoke (as opposed to a speculative) office building. The brief included the construction of a landscaped river wall and a public riverside walkway. Three main blocks, containing nine floors, step back from low-rise bunkers at garden level, rising in cold symmetry to a bow window, reminiscent of the river frontage at Charing Cross, but this time crowned with menacing concrete spikes. There is an equal proportion of dark-green-glazed curtain walling and precast pigmented concrete panels (each weighing 5–8 tonnes). It is the largest precast-concrete cladding contract to date in the uk.

The building is utterly impermeable – the façade allows no insight into the human activities inside. These appearances are by no means deceptive: built into the concrete framework is a 'Faraday Cage' – a mesh which prevents electromagnetic information from passing in or out of the building. An anonymous site has gained a theatrically ominous building – aptly enough, its neighbour to the west is the Nine Elms Cold Store.

ADDRESS Albert Embankment, London SE1
CLIENT Regalian Properties
STRUCTURAL ENGINEER Ove Arup & Partners
CONTRACT VALUE £125 million
SIZE 12,000 square metres (site area)
TUBE Vauxhall – Victoria Line
RAIL Vauxhall from Waterloo
ACCESS none

SOUTH LONDON

Terry Farrell & Company 1990–93

WATERLOO INTERNATIONAL TERMINAL

'The Gateway to Europe' is one of the longest railway stations in the world, with the capacity to handle up to 15 million passengers a year.

Five new tracks were set out by British Rail; these determined the geometry and shape of the whole scheme. The new building is made up of four components. At the bottom, a reinforced-concrete box accommodates the car park which spans the Underground lines and forms the foundation. On top of this sits a two-storey viaduct supporting the 400-metre-long platforms. This part must bear the weight of the 800-tonne trains and their braking force. Third, brick vaults beneath the existing station were repaired to accommodate back-up services. The fourth and most prominent component is the roof, though it absorbed only 10 per cent of the overall budget. It extends the full length of the trains, providing shelter like a vast scaly sleeve. It happily disregards the apartment and office blocks along its length, clipping the corners of any buildings that stand in its way.

The complex structure is essentially a flattened three-pin bowstring arch, distorted to follow the curve and changing width of the platforms. A series of diminishing compressive tubes is employed to cope with any movement. Pressed, profiled, stainless-steel tapered tubes define the bays and give expression to the lightweight structure. In order to avoid cutting 2520 panels of glass to size, at vast expense, a 'loose-fit' glazing system of overlapping standard-size glass sheets had to be devised with a concertina joint to deal with the twist in the structure.

ADDRESS Waterloo Station, London SE1
ROOF ENGINEER YRM Anthony Hunt Associates
TUBE Waterloo – Bakerloo, Northern Lines
ACCESS open; the interior is open only to travellers to Europe

Nicholas Grimshaw & Partners 1991–93

BRITISH AIRWAYS LONDON EYE

The largest observation wheel ever built, the British Airways London Eye differs from its predecessor, the Ferris wheel, in three ways: the passenger capsules are fully enclosed; they are on the outside of the wheel structure and are motorised; and the structure is supported by an A-frame on just one side. The design works like a bicycle wheel, the rim in compression and the spokes in tension. The wheel is kept in motion during operating hours to conserve energy (it will stop for wheelchairs or reverse for the faint-hearted).

The structure comprises three main parts: the capsules; the hub and spindle; and the rim. Each of the 32 capsules is made up of 32 glass panels (curved to a degree never attempted before) attached to a steel frame which also acts as the chassis on which the capsule rotates independently of the rim. Their 4-metre diameter was determined by the restrictions of road transport. The spindle at the centre of the wheel and the hub rotating around it are supported by two 60-metre-high tapered columns forming the A-frame with cables fixed into Jubilee Gardens to anchor the structure. The rim is made up of a triangular truss using 1600 tonnes of steel. Sixty-four cables run from the hub to the inner chord, keeping the rim at a constant distance from the hub. Sixteen cables are fixed to the outer chord to keep the wheel stiff as it rotates. A history of problems on suspension bridges revealed that rainwater adheres to cables and can change their vibration characteristics; these cables have one thread smaller than the others so that rain can run down a gully.

SOUTH LONDON

ADDRESS Jubilee Gardens, York Road, London SE1
STRUCTURAL AND SERVICES ENGINEER Ove Arup & Partners
SIZE 135 metres high
TUBE Waterloo – Bakerloo, Northern Lines
ACCESS adults £7.45, children £4.95. Call 0870 500 0600 (groups 0870 400 3005)

David Marks & Julia Barfield Architects 1999/2000

CENTAUR STREET

The brief called for the construction of a four-unit European-style apartment building combining the qualities of a loft with those of a London terrace, on a brownfield site adjacent to the railway viaduct leading from Waterloo International Terminal. Two ground-floor apartments have direct access to a small communal garden at the rear of the site, and two first-floor apartments have balconies and roof terraces with magnificent views over multilane railway tracks and into the mouth of Nicholas Grimshaw's Waterloo Terminal building (see page 106). A change in datum level down the centre of the building causes a split in level through the middle of each apartment, creating a shift in scale and change in proportion from one side of any one apartment to the other. Each of the four apartments is divided into a double-height 'living half', with a gallery slab, offset from a single-storey 'bedroom half'. Services are held in a central box with all sockets discreetly floor mounted. dRMM developed the section from a diagram devised by the client.

As the client states, 'at Centaur Street the site is a challenge of dimension and condition'. A mere 400 square metres, it is bordered by roads to north and south, and hugs the railway viaduct on one side and a line of trees from neighbouring back gardens on the other. With car-parking space at the rear of the site, access is from the railway side marked by an overhanging louvered glass box that creates a naturally ventilated external lightwell for the landings of the main communal stair. A similar double-height glazed casement distinguishes the north-facing elevation – this one to be used as a wintergarden for the first-floor apartment.

The overall architectural approach – a tight palette of materials and fine detailing – has been robustly and consistently executed. The concrete shell remains exposed on interior walls and is covered in a layer of insulation and aluminium sheeting on the outside. A rain-screen forms a lightweight veil around the entire envelope; a clip-on cladding system

deRijke Marsh Morgan 2002

devised specifically for this project from vertical aluminium mullions with horizontal bands of a durable and easily maintained American 'timber-effect' cement board.

At the time of writing all four apartments are about to be put on the market – the upper levels being fitted out with underfloor heating, walnut floors and pristine stainless-steel kitchens, while the lower floors remain as shells. Although these are essentially luxury apartments, this small development sets an exemplary precedent for urban housing on a modest scale and on an apparently unforgiving site. The scheme presents a new domestic architecture which greets its richly layered and dilapidated surroundings flirtatiously. It does not try to prettify them but it cannot help but flatter.

ADDRESS Centaur Street, London SE1

CLIENT Solid Space

STRUCTURAL ENGINEER Adams Kara Taylor

SIZE site area 370 square metres; total floor area of accommodatio 505 square metres plus 43 square metres communal circulation

TUBE Lambeth North – Bakerloo Line/Waterloo – Jubilee, Bakerloo Lines

ACCESS restricted

deRijke Marsh Morgan 2002

COIN STREET HOUSING
BROADWALL AND SITE B

A site with a unique social and political history was acquired in 1984 for £1 million from the Greater London Council by a group of Waterloo and Southwark residents calling themselves the Coin Street Community Builders. A separate housing association, the Coin Street Secondary Housing Co-operative, was subsequently set up to get funding to develop individual housing sites. Once a scheme has been completed, it is run by its own co-operative, drawing tenants of mixed incomes and origins from Lambeth and Southwark. All adults are made members of the co-operative, responsible for setting and paying rents to the Secondary Housing Co-operative.

Because of the poor quality of the detailing in the initial schemes, subsequent housing has been commissioned on the basis of architectural competitions. **BROADWALL** is the result of this policy. The brief called for 25 dwellings comprising ten family houses with gardens, five two-bedroom three-person flats and ten one-bedroom two-person flats. The layout of the scheme demonstrates a logical and effectively urban way to accommodate a mixture of people with different housing needs, addressing an ingrained scepticism towards building types such as the tower block.

The smaller flats for two people have been grouped together in a nine-storey tower at the north end of the site (the head); the flats may lack gardens but they do have a stunning view across the river. An elevator serves each floor individually for privacy and security. The neck and tail at the south end of the scheme is formed by two four-storey blocks for the larger flats; the main body is a row of 11 three-storey family houses with direct access to a new park on the west side of the scheme. All the flats and houses have spacious kitchens and living rooms with a western outlook through full-height windows, and balconies with enough room to sit out on. Bedrooms are located against the impenetrable brick wall on the street side.

SOUTH LONDON

Lifschutz Davidson 1995/Haworth Tompkins Architects 2001

COIN STREET HOUSING

A generous budget (80 per cent of which came from a Housing Corporation grant) allowed unusual attention to be paid to the quality of detailing, which uses a wide (some might say extravagant) selection of materials. This should increase the project's longevity although the scheme is too expensive to serve as a model for other housing-association developments.

The site sits at the heart of an architectural goldmine with Tate Modern (see pages 120–124), the reconstructed Globe Theatre (pages 130–132), the London Eye (page 108), and Southwark Station on the Jubilee Line Extension (page 322). It benefits from the new pedestrian and road route linking Blackfriars Bridge with the South Bank complex – a series of anonymous back streets has been transformed into a clearly defined avenue by new lighting, paving, bollards and flags designed by various artists.

SITE B is the Coin Street Community Builders' latest housing development. This scheme differs from previous CSCB housing developments by creating a courtyard plan that provides 32 family houses and a total of 27 flats and maisonettes grouped around a communal garden (taking the garden squares of Notting Hill as its precedent). The homes occupy three sides of a four-storey quad, with a community-facilities building expected to occupy the fourth side, subject to a second phase of development. The architect's ambition was to create a specific sense of place for residents on a very exposed site surrounded by large buildings of significant scale and ambition on one side and another housing development from the early 1980s of a similar scale on the other. The architectural vocabulary had to be understood by residents and passers-by in order to establish clear signals of public and private space.

The hollow square form is used more frequently for multi-storey apartment build-

SOUTH LONDON

Lifschutz Davidson 1995/Haworth Tompkins Architects 2001

COIN STREET HOUSING

ings where windows face outwards to the street and access is from the internal face. Here the street elevations sit quietly back from the pavement, defined by a pronounced formal brick screen containing gratifyingly large picture windows proudly revealing domestic interiors – there are few net curtains to be found here. The internal elevations are clad in timber to weather and mature with the landscaping. From the street, the building is understated to the point of being invisible. It is perhaps its invisible quality that is its strength, contrasting greatly with the neighbouring block with its primary-coloured gates and doors in the face of the street. Site B is not here to dazzle but to provide a safe place for those who live on a major urban thoroughfare, where everything around operates on a daily timetable, weekly performance programme or seasonal schedule. The best indication of its scale and focus of ambition is that each home has a roof-mounted solar panel for the production of domestic hot water.

SOUTH LONDON

ADDRESS off Stamford Street, London SE1

CLIENT Coin Street Secondary Housing Co-operative/Coin Street Community Builders

STRUCTURAL ENGINEER Buro Happold Consulting Engineers/Price & Myers

SIZE 27 units on a 0.15-hectare site (the whole site is 5.3 hectares)ss

TUBE Waterloo – Bakerloo, Northern Lines; Southwark – Jubilee Line

ACCESS none to individual homes; see the project from Stamford Street

Lifschutz Davidson 1995/Haworth Tompkins Architects 2001

TATE MODERN

In 1992, the Tate trustees announced their intention to divide the displays then held at Millbank between two sites. Millbank (renamed Tate Britain) would show British art from 1500 to the present day, while a second London gallery would display international modern and contemporary art. In 1995 the Tate sought to acquire Bankside Power Station but meanwhile continued its record of architectural patronage (having built Stirling's Clore Gallery in 1987, Tate Liverpool in 1988 and Tate St Ives in 1993) by holding an international competition to transform the building. It was won by young Swiss architects Herzog & de Meuron. Clearing and construction work began in 1996.

Bankside Power Station, designed by Sir Giles Gilbert Scott and built in two phases between 1947 and 1963, closed in 1981 – a short life for such a very large building. The steel structure clad in more than 4.2 million bricks was inspired by Dutch modernism, expressed in the swathes of masonry and the emphasis on verticality in the long slender windows. The distinctive central tower stands 99 metres high, designed to respond to the height restrictions imposed by St Paul's dome.

Herzog & de Meuron chose to reinterpret Scott's 'cathedral of pure energy' as a cathedral of light. The main elements of their design comprise vast light beams – one two-storey obscured-glass box rests on the full length of the roof of the existing structure, replacing the original shoulders of the building to either side of the tower. This element brings natural light into the top gallery spaces and acts as a beacon of the building's change in function. The plan of the building can be divided into three long sections. The central turbine hall is conceived as an internal street. An entrance at the west end funnels visitors down a long ramp into the belly (below ground and riverbed level) of the 35-metre-high volume. It is still recognisably an industrial space, retaining key elements such as a gantry crane (now used to lift large sculptures). A single mezzanine breaks the void

Herzog & de Meuron 2000

at ground level which brings visitors inside from the smaller riverside entrance on the north face. From here a low humming noise emanates from behind a sheer brick wall on the south side to let us know that a electricity substation is still operating there, waiting for future development. The section on the north side (formerly the boiler house) is dedicated to seven floors of gallery space and contains offices, shop, restaurants, members' and education rooms and an auditorium. A further two light beams or 'bay windows' form an internal façade between the turbine hall and the gallery block, creating a visual connection between the spaces and the light beam on the roof. Visitors are elevated to the level of the turbine hall's steel rafters with magnificent views down into the open space. The windows also act as intermediary spaces between the galleries and provide room to sit, read or contemplate.

The design of the galleries themselves has been determined by the dubious curatorial system which Tate Modern has instigated – a move away from the stratification of work by medium or school and towards a system that organises work by theme. This resulted in maintaining a minimum roof height of 5 metres throughout (except for one double-height space containing work by Joseph Beuys). Despite small variations in floor dimension, configuration and lighting, the galleries are surprisingly uniform in character, executed with the minimum of surface interruption and arranged on a regular grid plan. Walls are built to look permanent, though they can be moved.

The architects' overall approach to this magnanimous project has been to use broad brush strokes in both design and detailing. The new interventions retain the industrial in their scale and execution, but given the scale of the building no single element speaks out more loudly than any other – even the 'grand' steel staircase seems to become absorbed in the floor levels. Materials, including polished concrete and untreated green oak floors

Herzog & de Meuron 2000

in the galleries, are chosen to last and withstand heavy use. The architects are quick to point out that the flooring will look ghastly in five years but terrific in thirty.

The question remains whether the definition of a gallery for modern art in the twenty-first century would have been more appropriately answered in an entirely new building (cost factors apply) – conversions always throw up compromises. One gross example is the separately designated entrance for wheelchairs and buggy pushers via the café lest they gather lethal momentum on the ramp. Despite its commanding nature as a spatial device the ramp is unforgivably undemocratic; surely the pitch could have been analysed more thoroughly to provide access for all? The space carved out of Bankside is undeniably awesome, positively cathedral-like, and has overwhelmingly inspired visitors to enjoy the architectural experience as much as looking at the art. Similarly the gallery's presence (assisted by the new Jubilee Line station at Southwark) will provide a catalyst for regeneration in a beleaguered part of the city.

ADDRESS Bankside, London SE1
CLIENT Tate Gallery Projects
ASSOCIATE ARCHITECT Sheppard Robson Architects
STRUCTURAL AND SERVICES ENGINEER Ove Arup & Partners
CONTRACT VALUE £134 million
SIZE 34,000 square metres of gallery space
TUBE Southwark – Jubilee Line
ACCESS open Sunday to Thursday, 10.00–18.00; Friday and Saturday, 10.00–22.00

Herzog & de Meuron 2000

MILLENNIUM BRIDGE

'The Blade of Light' was the competition-winning entry designed by a collaborative archi-tect/artist/engineering team for a bridge to link the City of London at St Paul's Cathedral with its modern-day counterpart, the Tate Modern (then under construction), creating a new axis in the city. This pedestrian bridge proposes a new route from the West End to the City incorporating two river crossings (the other being at Hungerford Bridge). Concept drawings show a man with outstretched arms holding up a length of rope in each hand. This is the engineering principle which has informed the design – a very shallow suspen-sion bridge. The dramatic foreshortening of the vertical steel transverse arms was designed to fulfil the requirements of a 'blade of light'.

The bridge is 350 metres long and 4 metres wide. Two Y-shaped piers and a mere eight steel cables (four on either side of the platform) hold the bridge in position. Because of the low curve of the cables, the tension forces are very high. Deep abutments translate the tension from the cable anchor points to the 30-metre-deep piles penetrating north and south river banks. The elliptical piers and the curvature of the handrail are designed to minimise wind loading. Lighting is integrated into the structure rather than added on; a photocell turns it on at dusk and off at dawn. The police determined that the system should throw up enough light to illuminate walkers' faces to prevent crime but not to daz-zle and make the platform appear dim. Each feature enhances the feeling of lightness in the structure. A quick glance back up river to Blackfriars Bridge (1860–69) also serves as a good reminder of how bridge engineering has evolved ...

Or not. In particular, Foster's resolution of the Bankside landing which doubles back on itself engineers one last look at the bridge rather than carrying an anticipatory eye towards Herzog & de Meuron's Tate Modern. The bridge opened to the public on 10 June 2000; 150,000 people crossed it in the first three days. The rhythm created by the enthu-

Foster and Partners/Sir Anthony Caro/Arup 2000–01

MILLENNIUM BRIDGE

siastic walkers resonated with the natural frequency of the bridge and caused the platform to sway dramatically. As the people moved in time with the bridge, the sway increased. The bridge was closed two days later and remained so for more than a year. Detailed analysis of crowd movement and vibration was carried out at the Building Research Establishment using full-scale models and equipment usually employed in stadium design. Additional dampers were applied across the bridge (like shock absorbers) to dissipate the energy built up in the structure with minimal impact on the overall design. It reopened in February 2002, completing the splendid and continuous walk from Trafalgar Square, along the Strand, past Somerset House and along Fleet Street to St Paul's, across to Bankside, along the South Bank of the Thames and back over Hungerford Bridge.

ADDRESS approach from Bankside, SE1, or Queen Victoria Street, EC4
CLIENTS The Bridge Trust/Corporation of London/Southwark Borough Council
STRUCTURAL ENGINEER Arup
CONTRACT VALUE £18.2 million (at last count)
SIZE 1205 square metres
TUBE St Paul's – Central Line/Southwark – Jubilee Line
ACCESS open

Foster and Partners/Sir Anthony Caro/Arup 2000–01

GLOBE THEATRE

This is the oldest new building in London (even older than the British Library) and the first thatched building to be constructed in central London since the Great Fire of 1666. Its history dates back to 1598-99, when the original round wooden theatre was built by Cuthbert and Richard Burbage with master craftsman Peter Streete. The Globe was named after its sign, which showed Hercules carrying the world on his shoulders, not, as is often thought, because of its polygonal plan (suggesting a sphere) with the central pit around the stage open to the heavens. The theatre was destroyed in 1613 – it is thought by a cannon fired during a performance of shareholder William Shakespeare's Henry VIII, which set the thatch alight. It was rebuilt immediately on the original foundations but was closed by the Puritans in 1642 and demolished two years later.

The idea of rebuilding the theatre was resuscitated by actor Sam Wanamaker, who established the Globe Playhouse Trust in 1970. In the same year Southwark Council offered the trust this 1.2-hectare site, only 180 metres from the original. Seventeen years later the site was cleared and a diaphragm wall constructed to protect it from the River Thames so construction could begin.

Peter McCurdy's team worked for six years on the research, detailed design and fabrication of the timber structure using panoramic maps, illustrations of theatres of the period, and contracts, accounts and surveys of buildings of a similar date. From this analysis the diameter was established. Twenty bays form a galleried perimeter wall, each three storeys high and thatched in Norfolk reed with lime plaster. The stage in the centre is covered by a canopy spanning 14 metres supported on two 8.5-metre-high timber columns (made from trees found in the Scottish Borders and in Norfolk). Having completed 15 bays, work began on the stage and Tyring House (the backstage area). At this point the stage roof was redesigned in line with further research that suggested a larger,

Theo Crosby at Pentagram 1997

GLOBE THEATRE

projecting pentice roof and a more complex 'heavens' structure (the highly decorated ceiling above the stage).

Remaining true to sixteenth-century materials, the craftsmen used unseasoned green oak. The young timber is liable to move considerably as it ages, so each scribed joint is unique and identified with the carpenter's numeral, as would have been the case in 1598.

Can the process of faithful reconstruction inspire the way we approach contemporary buildings, or is it motivated by the 'Disney factor'? Unfortunately both the founder of the project, Sam Wanamaker, and the chief architect, Theo Crosby, died during the building process. However, master craftsman Peter McCurdy maintains that the building provides a unique forum for academic and archaeological research and investigation into the design and construction of timber frames as well as a platform for actors and audiences alike to explore a more authentic staging of Shakespeare's theatre.

ADDRESS Park Street, Bankside, London SE1
CLIENT The Globe Playhouse Trust
SPECIALIST CRAFTSMEN McCurdy & Co
STRUCTURAL ENGINEER Buro Happold Consulting Engineers
CONTRACT VALUE £30 million
SIZE 30.5 metres diameter, 91.5 metres circumference
TUBE London Bridge – Northern Line/Southwark – Jubilee Line
ACCESS open for performances

Theo Crosby at Pentagram 1997

THE JERWOOD SPACE

A Victorian red-brick school building has been restructured to provide a permanent gallery space, four dance and theatre rehearsal studios and five lettable studio spaces for artists and designers. Office facilities are attached to each rehearsal space so a small company can set up camp for the duration of its rehearsal time. The ground-floor spaces can be linked together and to the courtyard at the side through tall, partially glazed partition doors.

The client was keen to preserve as much of the original building as possible, while the limited budget meant that any new proposals had to focus on essential needs. So Paxton Locher's scheme is composed of broad brush strokes which make maximum use of space and natural light, and clarify use. The new main entrance and gallery occupy former bike sheds in the space linking the old flanking entrances on Union Street (the 'boys' and 'girls' keystones have been incorporated into outdoor benches). This long block makes use of original steel roof trusses and north-facing roof lights with the addition of an entirely glazed back wall facing on to an internal sculpture court. The client was concerned that the glazing would reduce the amount of hanging space within the gallery, so removable display panels have been designed to attach to the glazing panels when required. A café at the west end of the block also opens on to the planted courtyard.

Paxton Locher excel at exploiting deep awkward spaces without making them feel cramped or claustrophobic. Their strategy is to capture natural light sources wherever possible and create clear sightlines between spaces, using glass for walls rather than solid partitions. The method comes into play in the main office area, located at a difficult junction between the front gallery block and the rehearsal studios in the main body of the school. At some point a mezzanine level had been inserted into this area forming small box-like rooms. Now, with fully glazed partitions and the use of an existing exterior dou-

Paxton Locher Architects 1998

Jerwood
painting prize
1998

THE JERWOOD SPACE

ble-height window, the ground- floor reception and director's office on the mezzanine level both benefit from an unobstructed vista through to the gallery, courtyard and entrance.

The main body of the old building remains reassuringly raw, its robust features – high ceilings, tall windows, glazed-tile walls and scrubbed concrete corridor floors – preserved. An application for lottery funding at an advanced stage called for the provision of a lift for disabled access. Responding to the client's request for something 'butch', the architects have encased the east elevation in glass with gangways at first- and second-floor levels linking directly to a new brick and glass lift tower.

Reconditioning old buildings for new uses became something of a joke in the 1980s; a retained structure would be disembowelled to make way for new slab floors and suspended ceilings slung crudely across existing window openings. This project shows that a more intelligent approach may be taken and that some old buildings can benefit from a new lease of life.

ADDRESS 171 Union Street, London SE1
CLIENT The Jerwood Foundation (with financial assistance from the Arts Council Lottery Fund)
STRUCTURAL ENGINEER Elliott Wood Partnership
CONTRACT VALUE £500,000
SIZE 2300 square metres
TUBE Southwark – Jubilee Line
ACCESS gallery open 10.00–18.00 daily

Paxton Locher Architects 1998

DESIGN MUSEUM

The Design Museum was set up by Terence Conran and Stephen Bayley to explain the function, appearance and marketing of consumer goods. It also provides a resource to inform the work of the present-day design industry. It can be seen as a monument to the changing status of design during the Thatcher era. The objects in the museum are design classics which have now become cult objects – strangely contradictory.

The project started as the refurbishment of a disused 1950s warehouse overlooking the Thames but it proved cheaper to demolish and rebuild much of the original building because of a VAT ruling on all construction except new building in the 1984 budget.

The Study Collection is housed on the top floor in a double-height space saturated in natural light, which causes the neutral English oak and marble floors and white walls to glow. The temporary gallery is the usual adaptable white space. Both were designed by Stanton Williams. The Blueprint Café, designed by Terence Conran, is the only facility that really makes use of the original building and its location, by employing the layered frontage. The entrance, up a wide white stairwell, leads into the open café area with its glass frontage and terrace overlooking the Thames. The proximity of water and the coolness of the space make you feel like you could be dining luxuriously on a cruise liner.

The museum itself, once a red-brick building, now rendered and painted white, pays tribute to the simplicity of the modern movement. The café, on the other hand, is a product of Conran's quest to educate our ignorant British palates with Mediterranean cooking.

ADDRESS Shad Thames, London SE1
CONTRACT VALUE £5.1 million **SIZE** 3700 square metres gross
TUBE Tower Hill – Circle, District Lines, walk over Tower Bridge
ACCESS open daily, 10.30–17.30

SOUTH LONDON

Conran Roche 1987–89

LABAN DANCE CENTRE

Designed in collaboration with Michael Craig-Martin, this new home for a leading contemporary-dance institution includes dance studios, health facilities, a 300–seat theatre and lecture theatre and a public café. In an area that to date has only been given the chance to reveal its darker side, the Laban Centre has some very distinguishing features, none more so than the softly coloured polycarbonate cladding that shapes a vast semi-transparent lightbox, illuminating this not-so-light-industrial estate in Deptford. The quality of the exterior changes according to natural light levels – the busy internal life is partially visible outside by day, while at night the colour intensifies. This and the gentle concave 'cinemascope' curve of the front elevation broadcast the building's presence. But the Laban Centre is in no way divorced from its surroundings – the industrial-shed-like form has simply been put into gentler hands.

Inside, the staircase marks the entrance and serves as a bold sculptural reference point (a similar strategy is employed at Tate Modern, also designed by Herzog & de Meuron). On entering, one is greeted by a thick concrete corkscrew driving its way through the building. Painted black as tar, the plasticity of the concrete contrasts dramatically with the lightness of the exterior, both evoking aspects of the delicacy and dexterity of dance. Main corridor spaces are widened to form three internal streets running from the front to back of the plan, fully glazed at either end to frame views of lofty church spires beyond the creek. Clear glazing reveals every aspect of activity in the studios to passing staff and students.

ADDRESS Creekside, London SE8
STRUCTURAL AND SERVICES ENGINEER Whitby Bird & Partners
DOCKLANDS LIGHT RAILWAY Greenwich
ACCESS for information call 020 8691 8600 or visit www.laban.org

Herzog & de Meuron 2002

PECKHAM LIBRARY

Until recently there was little to entice an outsider to Peckham and, for residents, not much to relieve the tedium of a trip to the shops. However, today a new library stands as part of a new public square alongside the Arch and Pulse, a health and fitness centre designed by the council's own architects. The library is an heroic building, not only as part of Southwark's programme of regeneration, but also for reforming preconceptions of community architecture. Stirling Prize winner 2000, if there is one building in this book you must visit, this is it.

The building stems from a client brief to redefine the role of a library in the local community and illustrates a number of themes that preoccupy Alsop & Störmer. Long opening hours seven days a week are as critical to the design as the architect's own convictions that the public domain is enriched by strong form and colour, that seriousness of purpose does not preclude style or wit, and that by elevating the building it gains a sixth façade or underbelly and, thus, a peculiar presence.

An upturned L-shape rests on a handful of angled columns creating a covered arcade which anticipates the entrance to the library and extends the square outside. The north façade is fully glazed, with large patches of vividly coloured glass. Other exterior surfaces are clad in pre-patinated copper and steel mesh. The shape reappraises the conventional expectations of the building type. The slim vertical element is occupied by offices, meeting rooms, the elevator and ancillary facilities. The large elevated floor plan at fourth-floor level houses the library itself which benefits from quiet and a splendid quality of natural and tinted light inside (through skylights and the coloured glass) and dramatic views out. It leaves the street at ground level, for traversing and conversing. Nesting inside the library are a set of three pods on stilts containing a meeting room, a children's activity centre and an Afro-Caribbean study centre. The rooms are sound-insulated and lit from above

Alsop & Störmer 1999

PECKHAM LIBRARY

to make them magical, semi-secret spaces. The Afro-Caribbean study centre is shaded from above by the large red beret which perches on top of the building. The large polished hazelnut on the ground floor (serving as an office and interview room offering advice on council services) is a similar pod structure. The complex geometry of the timber forms was set out using 3-D software; softwood ribs are lined on either side with board forming a boat-type construction which allows for double-curved surfaces; an external skin of plywood tiles is stapled on to this. Many of the materials used in the building transcend the perceived hardness of their surfaces and become fabric in their appearance and texture, often as a result of inventing new ways to construct new forms.

While the building does not wear its environmental credentials on its sleeve, it is happily not air-conditioned. A combination of shading, natural ventilation and the passive cooling effects of its very elegant concrete frame combine to produce considerable energy savings. However, the large letters on the roof speak volumes; a place with books at its core, a building about exploration and discovery which elevates the mind and the spirit both metaphorically and literally.

ADDRESS 167 Peckham Hill Street, London SE15
CLIENT London Borough of Southwark
STRUCTURAL ENGINEER Adams Kara Taylor
SERVICES ENGINEER Battle McCarthy
CONTRACT VALUE £4.5 million **SIZE** 2300 square metres
RAIL Peckham Rye
ACCESS open Monday, Tuesday, Thursday, Friday, 9.00–20.00; Wednesday, 10.00–20.00; Saturday, 9.00–17.00; Sunday, 12.00–16.00

SOUTH LONDON

Alsop & Störmer 1999

DULWICH PICTURE GALLERY EXTENSION

The Dulwich Picture Gallery, England's first public art gallery, was designed by Sir John Soane and built in 1811. Having been bombed in 1944, it was subsequently restored in 1947–53. Set in landscaped gardens adjacent to Christ's Chapel, it has been acknowledged worldwide as a very beautiful (some say perfect) small gallery. Certainly its permanent collection – including some enigmatic sketches by Rubens and an impossibly luminous self-portrait by Rembrandt – represents some kind of perfection in itself. In formal terms the building might be described as a 'romantic' form of neo-classicism in that the architect refers to this style's motifs and materials but plays with them obsessively. The building seems to have been carved out of brick. With few actual window openings in the external elevations (and more blind arches added during refurbishment to create the additional internal hanging space), the brickwork appears to have been cut out to form ridges and recesses resulting in an expressive pattern of shadowing.

With the precedent for modernisation set by galleries and museums such as Tate Modern, Tate Britain and the Serpentine Gallery, the DPG also required refurbishment to upgrade its rooflights, to improve accessibility, lighting control, to create additional hanging space within the original building, reorganise the support facilities, and to create a new visitors' entrance incorporating a café, lecture/function room, an education room and a covered route between the new and old parts. A new single-storey brick building accommodates the café, function room and WCs. It is linked to the gallery by a glazed cloister forming a quadrangle to define the formal garden in front of the gallery – as was originally designed.

The steel-framed cloister is the key to the design. Bronze box columns support a stainless-steel brise-soleil to provide shading in summer; large sections of the glass open up in warm weather. Glass acts as an infill in areas where the structure meets existing

Rick Mather Architects 2002

DULWICH PICTURE GALLERY EXTENSION

buildings so that the new-built fabric floats off solid walls, mediating between architectural styles and admitting natural light into otherwise hidden corners. Although very pleasing as a building in itself (especially in really cold weather), problems arise in the cloister where levels change and sloping floors do not seem to have been resolved in relation to the delicate frame. I would have preferred to see the lawn or an adventurously planted border stretch along the edge of the base of the cloister instead of the rather self-conscious arrangement of large pebbles.

The 'education room' has been tucked into the side of Christ's Chapel feeding directly off the cloister. As I have requested elsewhere in this book – please find another name for this facility. I have yet to be convinced of its validity in any of the new gallery/museum refurbishments with its Victorian instructive connotations! What is wrong with 'studio' or 'workshop'? – both terms that at least suggest creative activity, making and exploration.

SOUTH LONDON

ADDRESS between College Road and Gallery Road, Dulwich Village, London SE21
CLIENT Dulwich Picture Gallery
STRUCTURAL ENGINEER Dewhurst Macfarlane & Partners
SIZE 1780 square metres gross
RAIL West Dulwich from Victoria (12-minute journey)
ACCESS open Tuesday to Friday, 10.00–17.00; Saturday, Sunday and bank-holiday Monday, 1.00–17.00

Rick Mather Architects 2002

HORNIMAN MUSEUM EXTENSION

The Horniman Museum was founded by Frederick John Horniman, a tea-trader, During the course of his travels he assembled a fine and eclectic collection ranging from stuffed animals to tribal masks, and clothing to musical instruments (the collection continues to grow). The original building was designed by arts & crafts architect Charles Harrison Townsend and constructed in red brick and stone. It opened in 1901 for the 'recreation, instruction and enjoyment' of the people. Subsequently the museum was presented with 8.5 hectares of gardens by the London County Council.

Like so many museums, the Horniman has been developed over the last century in an ad-hoc way, facilities being added when funds became available. Recent National Lottery funding and additional fund-raising have allowed the architects to clear away the unsatisfactory extensions and outbuildings and take a fresh approach with a new building that entirely re-orientates the museum towards the gardens (one of Frederick Horniman's original intentions).

The new building forms a third, barrel-vaulted, gable to the street elevation echoing the form of Townsend's buildings and his use of stone on the façade. Red brick appears in the flanking walls leading back towards the garden and the same bond as the old building has been used. The main entrance gate from London Road is located at this end of the building and leads visitors through to the new main entrance that now lies at the heart of the complex. A top-lit double-height space connects new and old. A naturally lit neutral space with white-painted walls lies between the museum interiors and the gardens outside. This building houses new galleries, an 'education area', a café and shop and improved access throughout the buildings.

The National Lottery has breathed new life into the nation's museums and their collections, many of which would have been beleaguered without it. This movement has pro-

Allies & Morrison 2002

duced a breed of well-mannered, contextual buildings that contribute more to spatial reorganisation than to a distinguished architecture in their own right. But this 'education area' is a peculiar misnomer. It seems to appear as a criterion in all 21st-century museum design. But surely that is the purpose of the museum galleries themselves and the joy of discovering their contents? The evolutionary diagrams painted as backdrops to each species of animal here are themselves more beautiful than any textbook image.

The approach here has to be compared to the generic and humiliating experience one had as a child of eating packed lunches in the 'school's room' in the bowels of one of the big museums on Exhibition Road – a space miraculously constructed from the stench of bleach and cheese-and-onion crisps. The Science Museum has confronted this issue in its Basement (see page 50). While that should serve as a precedent for all, it should not preclude a visit to the Horniman's strange and unexpected collection.

ADDRESS London Road, Forest Hill, London SE23
CLIENT The Trustees of the Horniman Museum
STRUCTURAL ENGINEER Whitby Bird & Partners
SIZE 2500 square metres
RAIL Forest Hill from London Bridge
ACCESS open daily, 10.30–17.30

Allies & Morrison 2002

CRYSTAL PALACE CONCERT PLATFORM

Like the fractured section of an alien spacecraft fallen to earth, the concert platform has lodged itself firmly in the grounds of Crystal Palace Park. It is as if on impact the vast shard of rusty steel had blasted a clearing in the trees and made a crater that became a lake and a perfect seating bowl for 8000 people. In fact, the bowl already existed as a feature in the park as laid out by Joseph Paxton in 1864 when his Crystal Palace, designed for the Great Exhibition of 1851, was moved here from Hyde Park.

Far from being spaced-out, the sculptural gesture is informed by an understanding of the richness of the romantic English landscape within the park, the nineteenth-century notion of a folly and the desire to make a thoroughly modern building that would be in harmony with the landscape. The architect identifies four principles that underlie the concept for the design: natural colour – the structure becomes an organic form through the patina of the untreated building materials which respond to the changing light and weather conditions; *gravitas* – permanence and belonging to the landscape expressed through the mass of a single material, Corten A steel; *levitas* – a lightness of composition that is sensitive to the landscape (the essential balance between the cantilevered acoustic reflector, the bulk of the accommodation module sitting on the concrete platform in the water and the monolithic speaker towers); and *simplicity* – a minimal intervention expressed in one continuous surface.

ADDRESS north-east corner of Crystal Palace Park, Sydenham Hill
STRUCTURAL ENGINEER Atelier One
ACOUSTIC ENGINEER Paul Gilleiron Acoustic Design
RAIL Sydenham
ACCESS open for performances during summer

Ian Ritchie Architects 1997

CAMDEN AND ISLINGTON

LONDON ZOO: RECENT ADDITIONS

London Zoo is a true 'architecture park' with no less than two Grade I-listed and eight Grade II-listed buildings, including The Mappin Terraces by Sir Peter Chalmers Mitchell and John James Joass (1913–14), The Penguin Pool (1934) and Round House (1932–33) by Tecton, the Elephant and Rhino Pavilion by Casson Conder & Partners (1962–65), The Snowdon Aviary by Lord Snowdon, Cedric Price and Frank Newby (1962–64) and a K-3-type telephone kiosk (a reinforced-concrete box, not the more famous red box) designed by Sir Giles Gilbert Scott. The original plan for the Zoological Gardens was prepared by Decimus Burton in 1827. The first animal enclosures were little more than cages, sheds and tents. The llamas were treated to a neo-Gothic house in 1828, and the Giraffe House was built in 1836; both buildings are still standing. It was not until later in the nineteenth century that attempts were made to make more of the enclosures appear attractive and not until the twentieth century that zoo design really began to allude to natural surroundings.

The latest spate of development at the zoo has been masterplanned by Wharmby Kozdon Architects with Dewhurst Macfarlane & Partners as engineers. This includes the Ambika Paul Children's Zoo (1995), The Camel and Llama House (1995) and The Web of Life (1999). The zoo's 'conservation in action' policy required that the sourcing of sustainable timber had to be in line with the World Wide Fund for Nature's guidelines (they recommend 50 per cent correct; here the architects achieved 90 per cent). Timber cladding is English green oak and a tropical hardwood from managed forests in Papua New Guinea. The Children's Zoo, intended as an educational facility for young children, houses domesticated animals from around the world. The architect's intention was to respond to the nature of this area's occupants and not compete with the more powerful architectural expressions of neighbouring structures. The plan is a series of paddocks connected by three main buildings facing both the zoo and Regent's Park: the Courtyard

Wharmby Kozdon Architects 1995–

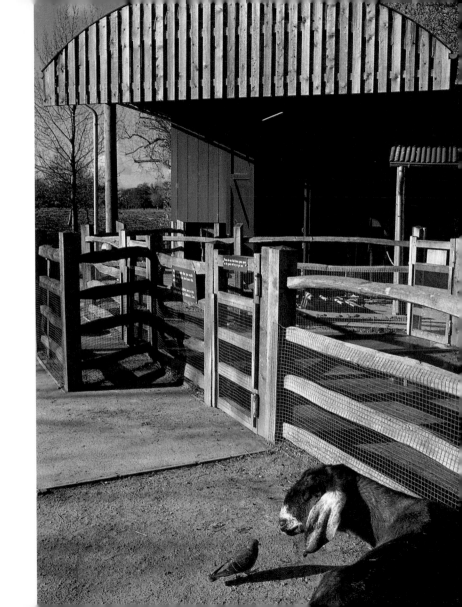

LONDON ZOO: RECENT ADDITIONS

Building, the refurbished Mess Building or Reindeer Den, and the Camel and Llama House. The main focus of the plan is the Courtyard Building, conceived as a traditional single-storey rough-pole barn with a corrugated-iron roof covering small pens and stables. The corner of the courtyard is anchored by the Pet Care Centre, an 8-metre cubed block used as a study room. Reindeer suffer from chronic dandruff which makes the Mess Building interesting. Ventilation is of the upmost importance so a recycled-polypropylene slatted roof was installed. The camels and llamas seem to like to eat their new building but no doubt they also appreciate the radial plan which takes in the extent of the paddock's perimeter fence and the timber arcade (the tasty bit) that shelters the animals' heads while supporting deep overhanging eaves. The timber roof is lined with moss for insulation. In the 1930s Pets' Corner was home to a chimpanzee, a lion cub, a small python, a baby yak and a giant tortoise, and hosted the Chimpanzees' Tea Party every afternoon. Today, The Touch Paddock is home to goats, sheep, rabbits, ducks and some cast-concrete animal-shaped lumps adorned with push-button-activated noises for when the residents decide not to perform.

The task of The Web of Life is to make biodiversity interesting to one million visitors a year and to provide research facilities. Designing for animals has few architectural leads in terms of building type and the architects felt that the zoo already had too many monuments. This building attempts to create a new concept in zoo keeping – a move away from a Darwinian classification of species housed in separate enclosures and towards the 'elemental and abstract' says the architect. It reverts to the shed structures that first occupied the site. A large roof made of Corten steel rests on regularly spaced Glulam timber columns forming a v-shape in plan. Overall stability is provided by cantilever columns. The glass walls create an open shelter for individual laboratories rather than an enclosure,

Wharmby Kozdon Architects 1995–

although the openness of plan is compromised by an already dated exhibition layout. Detached from the main structure are two smaller, cave-like spaces housing the WCs and children's activity room. They form a boundary for an entrance courtyard and take a slice through the earth, indicating the intention of the exhibit as a whole.

Again, impeccable green credentials were critical to the zoo's building policy. Foremost was the challenge to create a consistent internal environment (with a constant temperature of 21°C) for endangered species. A strong contribution to the building's character is the natural heating and cooling strategy devised by Fulcrum Consulting and expressed in the large chimney extractors on the roof. A heat exchanger recycles 80 per cent of the energy from outgoing stale air during cold weather, while warm-weather cooling is aided by the chimney extractors (warm air is drawn up and out) and water is supplied from a borehole. The resulting building is heaving with dynamic environmental activity on all levels from anteaters to wasps to control of solar gain. An expanding world needs to be reflected by an expansive architecture; this building refers to a fantasy farmyard vernacular with tentative attempts at enhancing a sense of scientific discovery.

ADDRESS Regent's Park, London W1
TUBE Great Portland Street – Circle, Hammersmith & City, Metropolitan Lines; Regent's Park – Bakerloo Line
ACCESS main zoo open 10.00–17.30 (last admission 16.30) daily. Check www.london-zoo.co.uk for details of special events

Wharmby Kozdon Architects 1995–

SADLER'S WELLS THEATRE

The first 'musick house' on this site was built in 1683 by Thomas Sadler and for five years acted as a side attraction to the medicinal well. The site's previous occupant before making way for the present theatre was designed in 1931 by F G M Chancellor with funds raised by Lilian Baylis as a north London home for her Old Vic Theatre Company. Once housing the Sadler's Wells Ballet, Sadler's Wells Opera and Sadler's Wells Royal Ballet (which moved out to become the Royal Ballet, 1946, English National Opera, 1968, and Birmingham Royal Ballet), the theatre – despite its cramped stage – has more recently maintained a year-round programme of dance, opera and lyric theatre.

The new building, completed using lottery funds, was designed to host touring companies, for commissioned new works of dance, opera and musical theatre and to nurture small companies over time. It now has a large performance stage (15 metres square) and a 26-metre-high flytower. But strict site boundaries and the retention of much of the existing steelwork of the circle seating determined that the overall scale remains largely unchanged.

The auditorium can vary its capacity from 900 to 1570 seats. The stage can be extended over the orchestra pit and the mesh panels covering four levels of gallery seating on the side walls can open to provide more seating or additional stage space, or close to be used as projection screens. The flying system (for scenery) is the first computerised system in the world and can drop a piece of flat scene from any one of its 75 bars at 1.8 metres per second to a dead stop.

The building brief emphasised the importance of taking an inclusive approach to access: disabled seating is the best in the house rather than stuck down in a corner at the front; textured floor surfaces, clear signage and generous corridor widths define main routes. The management is particularly proud of the generous provision of ladies WCs to

Arts Team @ RHWL with Nicholas Hare Architects 1998

SADLER'S WELLS THEATRE

cope with the interval rush. The backstage area is open for educational purposes and training and incorporates a community centre for lectures, a rehearsal space and a court-yard café for artists and staff.

The new Sadler's Wells is also a building for the visual arts, with advisers from the Royal Academy of Arts and gallery-owner Sadie Coles to assist in curating the public areas. The glazed four-storey space that forms the main foyer (and primary means of pub-lic circulation) on Rosebery Avenue uses switchable glass as a polyvision screen wall: transparent during the day to reveal day-to-day activities, it is opaque at night so visitors and passers-by can watch a display of moving and still images, adverts and programming.

English Heritage indicated that the former Grade II-listed building was listed for its historical significance rather than its architectural merit. The new building shell remains as profoundly undistinguished. The performance areas and facilities have undoubtedly been improved and stage and performers penetrating the realms of the auditorium are a challenge for any set designer, choreographer or director. But a brick-clad concrete frame with slices of planar glazing inserted at faintly deconstructed angles, adorned with a polyvision screen for a high-tech glow, is far from meeting the brief's claim that: 'The underlying concept for the design is innovation.'

ADDRESS 179 Rosebery Avenue, London EC1
STRUCTURAL ENGINEER Whitby Bird & Partners
CONTRACT VALUE £30 million
TUBE Angel – Northern Line
ACCESS foyer open – guided tours available at a charge

Arts Team @ RHWL with Nicholas Hare Architects 1998

THE BRITISH LIBRARY

The story is a long one – what St John Wilson calls the 'Thirty Years War' in his book *The Design and Construction of the British Library*. The book gives a personal account of the life of the project from the first proposals to relocate the British Museum's library and department of prints and drawings to a site between Great Russell Street and Bloomsbury Way in 1951, through the commission (with Sir Leslie Martin, who withdrew soon after the appointment) in 1962 and the many changes in government which hampered progress, to breaking ground in 1984 (on an entirely different site), to the present day when we can breathe a huge sigh of relief and say that the new British Library is open – well, phase I of III at least.

The British Library was created by an Act of Parliament in 1972 when the decision was made to unite the newspaper collections, science and patents departments and the humanities collections to make a single national library. Accommodating the entire brief on the proposed site proved impossible, so in 1973 9 acres of vacant British Rail land in St Pancras were acquired for the project. The election of a Conservative government in 1979 and an increasing disgust for contemporary architecture led to a bitter attack on the project. But, as St John Wilson states: 'that the project has survived the onslaught … must surely be proof of its fundamental necessity.'

The design principles derive from the mid-nineteenth-century English Free School. This 'school of thought', promoted by such architects as Augustus Pugin, Alfred Waterhouse and George Edmund Street, was generated in response to the need for an increasing variety of public buildings. These architects took a functional approach, allowing each building to develop according to its particular needs and through a free gothic form rather than employing classical Orders and conventions. Sir George Gilbert Scott's St Pancras Chambers (1867) next door is a superb example.

Colin St John Wilson and Partners 1997

These principles determined a 'from inside out' design approach. So the fundamental task from the outset was to gain a full understanding of the library's workings and the needs and aspirations of its occupants – despite a brief which stated that the building must have a working life of 200–250 years. The conflicting requirements produced different spatial patterns according to different types of use: for instance, whether a reading room is visited for long or short periods determines whether natural daylight is admitted from above or via perimeter glazing and therefore how the book stacks and reading tables are arranged. The common denominator is a 7.8-metre grid of columns. There are five and a half basement levels (reaching a depth of 24.53 metres below ground) and nine levels above ground, with reading rooms on the upper floors and storage and general public areas on the lower and ground floors. Variations on the grid are introduced through the vertical dimension, where bays can rise from one to three storeys high.

The building holds approximately 50 million items (books, maps, manuscripts, music scores and patents). The shelving stretches for 340 kilometres. At least 6.25 million records are searchable in the online catalogue, forever increasing. Orders for the book stores can be placed automatically from the catalogue and are delivered via the Mechanical Book Handling System to your desk within 30 minutes.

The most astoundingly elegant of the building's features – the six-storey bronze and glass Miesian vault that holds the Kings Library (George III's collection of leather- and vellum-bound books) – embedded in the centre of the main hall for all to revere (particularly from the restaurant). The cascading terraced effect of the entrance hall is echoed inside all the reading rooms on the west side, which are predominantly lit from above through clerestory windows and lantern lights. The side walls and floors of the entrance hall are of exposed brickwork (of the same stock in Leicestershire as St Pancras Cham-

Colin St John Wilson and Partners 1997

bers), a continuation of the external brickwork in the piazza. As one moves further into the building softer materials take over – travertine stone, polished brass, leather, American oak and carpeting.

The gulf between the sheer size of the building and the scale of its human users has been bridged by employing such devices as varied surfaces on which to sit, balconies on which to lean, short flights of steps and escalators, and visually breaking up large expanses of floor surface through a grid pattern in the stone and brick paving. Every detail from the readers' chairs to the book trolleys has been specially designed. All these factors have contributed to satisfy the fundamental requirement of any large public building – to make the public domain feel truly public.

ADDRESS 96 Euston Road, London NW1
CLIENT The British Library Board
STRUCTURAL ENGINEER Ove Arup & Partners
SIZE total gross floor area 112,643 square metres
TUBE Euston – Northern, Victoria Lines; King's Cross – Circle, Hammersmith & City, Metropolitan, Northern, Piccadilly, Victoria Lines
ACCESS piazza, foyer, shop, exhibition rooms, café and restaurant open Monday and Wednesday to Friday, 9.30–18.00; Tuesday, 9.30–20.00; Saturday, 9.30–17.00; Sunday, 11.00–17.00

Colin St John Wilson and Partners 1997

THE GREAT COURT AT THE BRITISH MUSEUM

The British Museum's Great Court was a lost space. The original museum of 1823, designed by Robert Smirke, was built to house King George III's library in four wings around a quadrangle. This space, fundamental to the plan, was soon filled with book-stacks and a rotunda accommodating the Reading Room (designed by Robert's brother Sidney in 1852), making it inaccessible to the public. Now the transfer of the King's Library and the contents of the Reading Room to the British Library has made it possible to open the court up again. The scheme intends to create a new civic space at the heart of the Heritage Route linking the British Library with the South Bank.

The first phase of construction was more archaeological dig than new building: the quadrangle was cleared of all structures except for the rotunda. This houses a restored Reading Room, open to all visitors, giving access to the 25,000-volume collection via a multimedia system. The rotunda itself has been enlarged on the north side with a bulge to accommodate exhibitions, a restaurant and shops. The internal façades of the quadrangle have been restored in a similar vein to Foster's route to the Sackler Galleries at the Royal Academy (see page 78), preserving the original building as a museum exhibit. However, the glazed canopy which covers the courtyard provides a contemporary intervention that serves to protect the past and frames an inspiring vision of the future. A fusion of state-of-the-art engineering and economy of form, its geometry is designed to span the irregular gap between the dome of the Reading Room and the line of the courtyard's façades.

Smirke's building is based on the limits of the technology of his time: load-bearing masonry. Its spanning limitations and the rules of proportion of Georgian architecture related the sizes of rooms to the dimensions of their windows in order to admit a good amount of daylight. The Reading Room was built when Victorian engineering offered new possibilities: the structure is a frame of cast and wrought iron with brick in-fill.

Foster and Partners 2000

THE GREAT COURT AT THE BRITISH MUSEUM

The strategy for the glass roof was to create a delicate structure with maximum transparency, avoiding the need for columns – it spans a distance of 100 metres by 70 metres. 800 tonnes of steel box beams are joined at 6000 individual six-way nodes, supporting 3312 triangular glazing panels, each of which is unique. During construction the tolerance between each structural node was just 3mm. Where it meets the Reading Room, the roof is supported by a ring beam and 20 composite steel and concrete columns which align with the original frame. In turn the columns are concealed with a new skin of limestone surrounding the entire drum of the Reading Room, the exterior of which was not intended to be seen. Two broad staircases encircle the drum, giving access to the upper levels. At the perimeter the roof is supported by Smirke's load-bearing walls.

The Great Court is the largest enclosed courtyard in Europe. Finally, along with projects such as Tate Modern and Peckham Square, architects, planners and clients are realising that the unpredictable British climate requires enclosed or covered public spaces if the population is expected to leave their homes for more sociable pursuits. Married with the initiative to keep these areas open from early in the morning until late in the evening, London may become a safer and more hospitable city, regardless of truth to materials.

ADDRESS Great Russell Street, London WC1
STRUCTURAL AND SERVICES ENGINEER Buro Happold Consulting Engineers
CONTRACT VALUE £98 million **SIZE** 6100 square metres
TUBE Tottenham Court Road – Northern and Central Lines/Holborn – Piccadilly and Central Lines
ACCESS open Monday to Wednesday, 9.00–21.00; Thursday to Saturday, 9.00–23.00; Sunday, 9.00–18.00

Foster and Partners 2000

9/10 STOCK ORCHARD STREET

There is nothing obviously beautiful about this site lying low behind a steel and willow gate at the end of a truncated row of terraced houses in north London, crudely hacked off to make way for bigger roads and railway tracks, a mass earth-moving exercise carrying on beyond – diggers and dumper trucks preparing the ground for a waste exchange and large high-rise housing development. However, 'this site' contains a building of immense curiosity if not of immediate beauty – it is the home and offices of architects Sarah Wigglesworth and Jeremy Till. The building's nature developed from many conversations and a sharing of stories between the two, rather than by the production of drawings. A tour around the house and offices embodies this idea of a continuous dialogue between inventor/maker and builder/occupant .

The L-shaped plan comprises an office wing, main living space and bedroom wing. The transition between home and work is via the dual purpose dining/conference room at the corner of the plan. The three-storey office block (forming the foot) is raised on gabions, vast cages filled with recycled concrete rubble (more commonly used in civil-engineering works) and is located nearest to the railway tracks. Deep pebbles surround the gabions at ground level creating an undercroft entrance, part beach, part railway siding. The trackside elevation is made up of a sandbag wall – a construction technique more associated with the Blitz than a contemporary office building. Bags are filled with a mixture of sand, concrete and lime and then tied back to a timber frame. Over time the cloth will perish (indeed it has done so faster than expected) to leave a rippling concrete wall. Found railway sleepers form necessarily substantial window frames in this wall. A quilted surface made from three layers of silicone-faced fiberglass swaddles the end and inward-facing elevations in final defiance of all conventional notions of the male-dominated workplace.

Two rows of round steel columns lift the main living space of the house above

Sarah Wigglesworth Architects 2001

ground level and march westwards to the back of the site. Its south-west facing aspect called for a maximisation of glazing to harness natural light and heat from the sun (which in truth has been over-estimated by approximately 25 per cent – this will be addressed by fixed external shading). The ad-hoc arrangement of glazing panels is the result of the double-pitched roof: at its highest point over the dining/conference room, it slopes down low over a more intimate kitchen-snug area – like a delicate Japanese tea-house colliding with a gardener's cold-frame. However, the extent of the glazing affords terrific views of large skies above and the large garden below which occupies almost half of the site (a garden being the most sustainable aspect of any built project).

Central to the open living room are two features that break the space (or what the architects describe as 'fruitful domestic clutter'): the larder, a naturally ventilated self-supporting brick beehive structure rendered with lime plaster, and what will eventually become the vertical library. A collection of vast steel columns that currently form a forest in the main living area will house a staircase and bookshelves rising up through the ceiling into the funnel-shaped tower that is the beacon for the building as well as part of its natural ventilation system. It will also provide access to the grass-covered roof, which thanks to its steep pitch is looking promisingly like a hillside meadow in the middle of a scarred urban landscape.

A plywood drawbridge leads those who are permitted from the main room into the private quarters of the bedroom wing; a straw-bale house. In fact the straw-bale wall continues along the entire rear north wall of the house, hence the fantastically warm, dry scent of harvest and unusual acoustic cushioning which pervades the house and intensifies as you reach the bedrooms – or, rather, burrows. Interior walls are rendered with lime plaster and sheets of steel and polycarbonate cladding form an external rainscreen.

Sarah Wigglesworth Architects 2001

9/10 STOCK ORCHARD STREET

Straw-bale construction has existed for at least 300 years. Like the sandbags, the materials and techniques employed are inexpensive but so long forgotten that they have had to be reinvented here.

The wide-ranging and unlikely materials employed in construction have been used because they are immediate and accessible. They express a glorious irreverence towards the traditional preoccupations of the profession: those of refinement, catagorisation and completeness – the RIBA would not offer this project an award because the building is in their eyes 'incomplete'. Rather, the house is still living and breathing. One is struck by how very big it is. This is not a sensible use of space, but it is a very human use of space. Part farmhouse (access to the house is solely through a back door), part allotment, part modernist villa, part castle, part bunker – it welcomes all these labels in a quizzically English manner.

ADRESS 9/10 Stock Orchard Street, London N7
CLIENTS Sarah Wigglesworth and Jeremy Till
STRUCTURAL ENGINEER Price & Myers
PROJECT MANAGER Martin Hughes
SIZE site 800 square metres; house 280 square metres; office 250 square metres
TUBE Caledonian Road – Piccadilly Line
ACCESS restricted – this is a private house with occasional open days. For group bookings email mail@swarch.co.uk

Sarah Wigglesworth Architects 2001

WHITE CUBE GALLERY EXTENSION

The design of this vertical extension above a former warehouse was determined primarily by the fact that any construction programme had to be carried out while the gallery (already occupying the ground and some of the first floors) was closed for its summer holidays. A series of steel beams replaced the old roof and provided a bed for new floors.

With a history of engineering mobile buildings needing swift assembly and dismantling, Atelier One helped to develop a lightweight, steel-framed modular structure. It was designed and built in 14 weeks, off-site in a Manchester factory. A procession of 18 units arrived on trucks on a wet August morning and were craned on to the roof . The process took four days (despite bad weather) and only a few more to connect up the cabling and services which run along one side of the building behind removable ceiling panels. It took a further month to open the extension while the more traditional works relating to the old building, such as connecting staircases and plastering of ceilings, were completed.

The two-storey glass box (happily more shoebox than perfect cube) is double-glazed on the street elevations and sealed with insulated plywood and sand-blasted glass skin on the rear elevations. Floors are plywood stitched to steel mesh (for lightness), lined with an acoustic mat and tongue-and-groove chipboard. A seamless resin floor was poured throughout, erasing any notion of the modular. The box is mechanically heated and ventilated in order to protect the art. Its presence looms light and large over Hoxton Square.

ADDRESS Hoxton Square, London N1
STRUCTURAL ENGINEER Atelier One
SIZE total gallery space 1000 square metres
TUBE Old Street – Northern Line
ACCESS open Tuesday to Saturday, 10.00–18.00

CAMDEN AND ISLINGTON

M J Rundell & Associates 2002

HAMPSTEAD

LISSON GALLERY

The Lisson Gallery is like a section of the street stripped bare. Each of its four storeys strictly corresponds in height to those of the neighbouring buildings. But the façades of the ground- and first-floor galleries have been peeled away to reveal the guts of the building through floor-to-ceiling-height square glass panels which can slide back to enable large works to be moved in and out of the gallery. The second and third storeys are occupied by flats with sheer concrete façades to allow some privacy from the school playground across the street.

Each of the basement, ground and first floors provides a 7-metre-squared space linked to the others by an atelier-type stairway to the side. This arrangement allows smaller shows to be exhibited in a single space or for full retrospectives to flow around the entire building. The route begins in the side entrance of the old Lisson Gallery on Lisson Street, which is linked to the new space by a long reception corridor. The journey becomes a succession of discoveries, exiting on to the adjacent Bell Street. This 'possession of the space by the visitor', as Fretton calls it, makes the gallery an integral part of a varied community, helping to break down the prejudices on which many art galleries thrive.

ADDRESS 52 Bell Street, London NW1
CLIENT Lisson Gallery London Ltd
STRUCTURAL ENGINEER Price & Myers
CONTRACT VALUE £500,000 approximately
TUBE Edgware Road – Circle, District, Hammersmith & City Lines
ACCESS open Monday to Friday, 10.00–18.00; Saturday 10.00–13.00

Tony Fretton Architects 1990

LORD'S CRICKET GROUND

Lord's has hosted a succession of pavilions since the first one-roombuilding was erected c 1820 (it burned down five years later during a Harrow v Winchester match). Today the ground is surrounded by eight pavilions or stands, the oldest of which is Thomas Verity's colonial-style pavilion (1899–90) on the west side flanked by the Allen and Warner corner stands (1958). The Tavern Stand (1966) sits next to the Mound Stand (1987) on the south side and the Edrich and Compton Stands (1991) make up the east side of the ground. The Grand Stand (1998) occupies the north side, replacing one built in 1926 and increasing the number of seats by more than 50 per cent to an overall ground capacity of 30,500. The most recent addition, the Media Centre (1999), looms over the east end of the ground.

At the end of the 1980s several architectural journals nominated the **MOUND STAND** (Michael Hopkins & Partners) as the 'best' building of the decade. Perhaps this is because it incorporated three diverse building techniques: the restoration and completion of a brick arcade built by Thomas and Frank Verity in 1898 at ground level, the cantilevered steel-framed decks above, and the tent structure of the roof. The tented roof harks back to that quintessentially English scene – the marquee on the village green. However, the technology employed is more reminiscent of the rigging on a boat: six vertical masts and a series of projecting steel booms with steel cables that tie down into concrete piles at the back of the stand and on to the front of the cantilevered deck to achieve overall stability. One of the pleasures of the building is that there was no need to insulate it or to make the decks watertight as it is only fully occupied on eight fair-weather days of the year. If it should rain, spectators can shelter under the huge Verity arches while members and their guests promenade on the top deck.

On the opposite side of the ground is the sleek outline of the **GRAND STAND** (Nicholas Grimshaw & Partners). It features a single central flagpole as the expression of

various architects 1987–99

a structure that puts an emphasis on horizontality with an almost invisible means of support. In fact, three columns support a two-storey spine beam, which in turn supports the upper tier. All vertical circulation is at the rear where staircases are cantilevered out to meet a screen of trees at the boundary wall, forming a type of arcade. The high degree of prefabrication used to control quality and for efficiency during tight construction schedules is reflected in the graceful composition of the building. It seems to have been lowered on to the ground rather than built up from it, appearing to hinge and unfold from the central column and mast.

The **MCC INDOOR CRICKET SCHOOL** (David Morley Architects) stannds to the east of the main ground. The dual aspects of 'learning' and 'enjoying' are expressed in the 'double-sided pavilion' plan: the clubhouse area is integrated into the front of the steel-columned training building, affording sheltered views of the school on the south side and overlooking the practice ground to the north. The floor is a concrete slab lined in a specialist surface called Uni-Turf Vinyl Sheet. The barrel-vaulted roof relates to the module of nets below and incorporates these into its structure. A system of partial glazing on the east-facing side of each vault combined with swathes of fabric-louvred blinds diffuses the sunlight. The building is unostentatious and complements the stands and pavilions in the ground.

The **MEDIA CENTRE** (Future Systems) is the latest addition. The architects drew their inspiration from the form of a camera (for framing the commentator's views) and the latest equipment and protective clothing of athletes. The result is a pod raised 14 metres above ground on two concrete service-tower legs. The building provides facilities for 250 journalists and photographers with broadcasting studios. Rather than a conventionally clad structure, the plan was to fabricate a semi-monocoque aluminium form (i.e. the

structure is in the shape). This approach was chosen because the aluminium will not corrode and can be formed to make a waterproof structural skin requiring no frame. Also, the form creates an unobstructed interior space. Made in 26 sections out of 6mm and 12mm sheet with ribs and spars to hold the form, the pieces were bolted and welded together on site. The exterior surface has been sanded and sprayed white for a seamless finish. The vast glazed wall overlooking the cricket pitch is made of toughened glass, inclined at 25 degrees to prevent any reflections on to the pitch.

The Media Centre is a one-off building. However, the practice is 'keen to explore the potential application of some of its technical and sensual attributes in ... something that is genuinely mass-produced'. Being that most retro of forms, the pod-shaped building represents the notion of a desire for things futuristic rather than being the consequence of an appropriate use of technology. The disparity between the form, adaptation of traditional manufacturing processes (this type of shell would be more efficiently made in fibre-reinforced polymers than in metal)and the environmental control of the finished building puts the Media Centre in the realm of the futuristic rather than in the future.

HAMPSTEAD

ADDRESS St John's Wood Road, London NW8
TUBE St John's Wood – Jubilee Line
ACCESS tour information on 020 7432 1033

various architects 1987–99

MILL LANE GARDENING PROJECT

In 1962 Walter Segal was confronted with the problem of providing temporary accommo-dation for his family while their house was being rebuilt. At a materials cost of £800 (£6500 today) and completed in two weeks, the first Segal self-build 80-square-metre house still stands in the garden of the Highgate house. The key to the success of the building was the rigorous simplification of the construction process: one person with basic carpentry skills could carry out the work (with perhaps the exception of services and roofing). Segal's system is based on a modular grid determined by the sizes of standard materials – ideally these could be disassembled and resold. The frame is timber, clad in woodwool and faced with roofing felt on the exterior and chipboard waste paper inside. The roof is flat (avoiding the use of scaffolding), surfaced with felt and held down by bricks and 35mm of water. Over 30 years later, the building would still pass tests for water penetration or structural failure. Details such as using stainless- rather than mild-steel bolts and timber jointing rather than nail-plate joints (too much movement) have been adopted by many subsequent schemes.

Five per cent of new housing stock in Great Britain is accounted for by self-build – the figure would be far greater if the political establishment could learn to appreciate the method's merits. Homes can be built for about one-third of usual cost. The Walter Segal Self-Build Trust was set up in 1988 to continue Segal's work after his death in 1985. The trust's aim is to help people with limited means to build themselves homes or community projects such as Mill Lane. What was intended as temporary accommodation has devel-oped into forms of permanent housing where families can build their own environments from start to finish, led by their own programme and with the ability to extend and change it as they wish.

The Mill Lane Gardening Project is a centre for adults with learning difficulties. The

Simon Yauner Architects 1992

MILL LANE GARDENING PROJECT

land is owned by Camden Council but had been deserted for years. A corner of the site was allocated to csmh for a gardening project. By the end of 1992 the trainees and a number of volunteers had acquired more than just green fingers. The building of the centre was carried out by the users themselves so that the construction process became an integral part of their training. Simon Yauner and his engineer, Rene Weisner, developed the design: discontinuous construction allowing movement between layers. Stephen Backes, a carpenter and welder, was employed to supervise the site and train the volunteers and trainees in basic building skills. Electrical and plumbing works were sub-contracted.

This seems to have been a rewarding process for everyone involved. The method opens a door on an architectural philosophy which isn't about monumentality; trainees gained confidence and learned skills (being prompt was high on Backes' agenda) which opened another door labelled 'anything is possible' ... as long as you turn up on time!

For details of other current schemes, contact The Walter Segal Self-Build Trust, 57 Chalton Street, London NW1 (020 7388 9582).

ADDRESS 160 Mill Lane, London NW6
CLIENT Camden Society for People with Learning Difficulties (CSMH)
STRUCTURAL ENGINEER Trigram Partnership
CONTRACT VALUE £70,400 (excluding architect's and engineer's fees)
SIZE 169 square metres
TUBE Kilburn – Jubilee Line
ACCESS open (but introduce yourself to whoever is around when you arrive)

HAMPSTEAD

Simon Yauner Architects 1992

THE CITY

LLOYD'S OF LONDON AND LLOYD'S REGISTER OF SHIPPING

Although it could barely be classified as 'recent' in relation to the other projects in this book, Lloyd's of London remains a modern architectural benchmark in this city and one of the greater projects to come out of the offices of the Richard Rogers Partnership.

This is not a tower block – it is rarely perceived as a whole. Rather, one glimpses bits of gleaming steel, or electric-blue light at night, patched on to the sober City landscape. Its proximity to other buildings allows it physically to penetrate its surroundings. The configuration is a result of its location within the medieval street pattern and the philosophy of the architect that the building should appear to be assembled from a 'kit of parts'.

The main structure is remarkably simple in plan: a stack of 'O'-ring floors (varying in level from six to 12 storeys) carried on central concrete columns and braced external columns creates a support for the vast tubular-steel lattice framework of the 70-metre-high central atrium. Six precast-concrete satellite service towers cling, structurally independent, to the exterior of the main frame. The tower is surmounted by five stunning electric-blue cranes. All the structural details are fully on display.

Inside, the atmosphere is awesomely cathedral-like. The focus for activity is the underwriting room (the Room) on the ground floor and first three mezzanine levels. 'Boxes' – flexible work terminals – were developed as kits by Tecno. Light pours into the canyon-like atrium space and additional light comes from large fittings, which also act as air extractors, set into the ceiling. The triple-glazed external cladding skin acts as an air duct from ceiling to floor. The building is functionally and aesthetically a living and breathing machine.

The RRP/Lloyd's oeuvre has more recently been updated at the new headquarters for Lloyd's Register of Shipping down the road in Fenchurch Street. With almost a 25-year gap between the two buildings, we can see how RRP have refined and rationalised their

Richard Rogers Partnership 1978–86/2001

design and construction process. The new building steps up from six to 14 storeys and incorporates an existing Grade II-listed building (1901) that has been restored as part of the scheme.

Main access is through a churchyard. A fan-shaped grid of tapered floorplates around two atrium spaces fits into the awkward geometry of the site. Two circulation towers face the churchyard with two secondary service cores containing WCs, goods lifts and staircases located at the rear. Key structural and circulatory elements are colour-coded: blue for the main structure, yellow for stairs, red for lifts. The glass envelope achieves ultra-transparency, revealing the workings of the building and its inhabitants' movements within. A façade system of rotating louvers, controlled by photo-cells located on the roof, maximises daylight while minimising solar-heat gain.

RRP are masters at detailing every nut, bolt and washer, staircase and concrete finish impeccably, but then, as one critic suggested, 'they jolly well should be by now'.

LLOYD'S OF LONDON
ADDRESS Lime Street, London EC3
STRUCTURAL ENGINEER Ove Arup & Partners
CONTRACT VALUE £169 million
SIZE 47,000 square metres
TUBE Monument – Circle, District Lines
ACCESS only by booking in advance; telephone 020 7623 7100

LLOYD'S REGISTER OF SHIPPING
ADDRESS Fenchurch Place, London EC3
STRUCTURAL ENGINEER Anthony Hunt Associates
SERVICES CONSULTANT Ove Arup & Partners
SIZE 34,000 square metres gross/24,154 square metres net
TUBE Monument – Circle, District Lines
ACCESS restricted

Richard Rogers Partnership 1978–86/2001

BRACKEN HOUSE

Bracken House was the Grade II-listed home of the *Financial Times*, built by Sir Albert Richardson in 1959. The dispersal of the newspaper industry throughout the 1980s left many valuable sites in the City empty, to be converted into London bases for American and Japanese banks. The old FT building had two office-block wings linked by an unspectacular octagonal printworks. It was this part that Hopkins demolished and readdressed.

A new oval plan has been sandwiched between the old wings. None of the old building was at right angles to the site, whereas the Hopkins doughnut has been set parallel to Friday Street so it bulges out as if being squeezed. The plan is centred on a rectangular atrium containing lifts with glass-brick walkways all around to allow light to filter into the office floors. At the corners are hollow, wedge-shaped columns which house services.

Each floor is open plan with a 4-metre-deep rim marked by secondary columns. This rim is crucial to the nature of the façade. The brief was that the façade should be long-life, low maintenance and structural and should refer to the materials of the old building. Load-bearing piers are of solid Hollington stone. The bay-window panels rest on huge three-armed brackets, also load-bearing, made of gun-metal. In the event of a fire the floor beams in the 4-metre span act as cantilevers so no added fire protection was required.

Bracken House is technically very creative and materials have been tested beyond decorative roles, but on the face of it, it is heavy and rather dreary. Not only is it squeezed from the sides, but St Paul's has squashed it with its big foot too.

ADDRESS 1 Friday Street, London EC4
STRUCTURAL ENGINEER Ove Arup & Partners
TUBE Mansion House – Circle, District Lines
ACCESS none

Michael Hopkins & Partners 1989–91

NO. 1 POULTRY

Poultry is named after the poulterers who used to live here before the street was demolished in 1817 because of the filth and stench that emanated from the local prison. No. 1 lies at the confluence of eight streets that lead to Sir John Soane's Bank of England (1788–1808). Other distinguished neighbours include Sir Edwin Lutyens' Midland Bank Head Office (1924–39) on the opposite side of the street, Sir Edwin Cooper's National Westminster Bank (1930–32) on the corner of Poultry and Princes Street, and the Mansion House (1739–52) on Walbrook designed by George Dance the Elder as the official residence of the Lord Mayor.

The site was formerly occupied by the Mappin & Webb building (1870) designed by J & J Belcher in the high-Victorian neo-Gothic style. In the late 1960s property developer Peter Palumbo submitted plans to demolish the building and replace it with a 1967 design for a modernist steel and glass tower surrounded by a pedestrian plaza by Mies van der Rohe. The proposal was refused planning permission by the then Secretary of State, though this did not 'rule out redevelopment of the site if there was an acceptable proposal for replacing existing buildings.'

Proposals were revived in 1985. Mies had since died, and James Stirling Michael Wilford & Associates, having recently completed what has since become a post-modern icon – the celebrated Staatsgalerie in Stuttgart (1977–82) – were commissioned to work on a new scheme containing offices, shops and public spaces. In 1988 a scheme was approved, followed by over two years of legal argument and soothing of public emotions over the proposed demolition of seven listed buildings. Construction finally began in 1994.

In true postmodern style, Stirling's building adheres to the existing street pattern and incorporates symbolic references to surrounding buildings, while the winged clock

Stirling Wilford Associates 1998

NO. 1 POULTRY

tower harks back to the Mappin & Webb building's circular turret. Construction techniques are also post-modern: a thin veneer of sandstone and granite clipped to a steel frame with a Playschool palette of colours applied to window frames and balustrades.

There are shops at basement and ground-floor levels and a pedestrian passage punctures the plan, linking shopping colonnades on the two main street frontages with an open courtyard at the centre which provides access to Bank Underground. The courtyard void, circular at ground- and first-floor levels, becomes a triangle when surrounded by the upper office floors, which are surmounted by a roof garden and restaurant.

Completion of truly significant buildings in London, for instance the British Library (see pages 170–174), is often so prolonged that they become a crystallisation of the moment when the first notion of their being hit the drawing board. This makes it difficult to compare them with other buildings – it's rather like comparing cave paintings with graffiti without taking into account the evolution in between. Ultimately No. 1 Poultry is London's postmodern flagship, designed by one of the world's leading proponents of that style. Today we can be happy for its contribution to the texture of our architectural heritage, though back in the 1980s one might have cast a more sceptical eye.

ADDRESS 1 Poultry, London EC2
CLIENT City Acre Property Investment Trust & Alstadtbau Ltd
STRUCTURAL ENGINEER Ove Arup & Partners
SIZE net area 13,117 square metres
TUBE Bank – Central, Northern Lines
ACCESS restricted within main development; restaurant on top floor open

Stirling Wilford Associates 1998

88 WOOD STREET

This office building is the result of a convoluted development process that took 11 years. When Daiwa Securities acquired the site it was occupied by a listed 1920s' telephone exchange. Its core chamber held cabling for much of the City so could not be removed. Between 1992 and 1995 the project was put on hold as the Japanese economy slumped; on resuscitation net lettable space was increased from 18,000 to 24,000 square metres within the same shell. In 1998 Daiwa decided not to move in and 88 Wood Street is still to be let.

The building rises in three linked steps of ten, 14 and 18 storeys, sympathetic to the heights of surrounding buildings and strategic views across London. The steps narrow as they get higher with the broadest, lower block facing on to Wood Street. The red and blue ventilation funnels which pop up from the pavement and the bright yellow steelwork are clues as to who designed the building (Pompidou Centre, Millennium Dome). It is difficult not to compare it with the Lloyd's Building (completed 14 years earlier). The most significant difference is the lack of exposed services here. With maintenance costs at Lloyd's proving astronomical, the architects have employed ultra-transparent glass and have specified the minimum of framing to seal the structure while allowing the building's intestines to remain visible. The inside benefits from almost frameless views out with a tracery of ducts, slender steel columns and lift shafts laid over the panorama. Such transparency puts even greater emphasis on detailed design.

ADDRESS 88 Wood Street, London EC2
STRUCTURAL AND SERVICES ENGINEER Ove Arup & Partners
CONTRACT VALUE £55 million **SIZE** 22,600 square metres
TUBE St Paul's – Central Line
ACCESS none

Richard Rogers Partnership 1999

LUDGATE

Ludgate is like a baby Broadgate (see pages 220–224), one-sixth its size and 30 per cent cheaper to build. Although from the same stable (Rosehaugh Stanhope Development), it is a more mature development. Conceived during the building mania of the mid-1980s, Ludgate has benefited from the necessity of trimming costs in the early 1990s. The buildings have become less ornate (less expensive tack) and more functional in plan and appearance, making them easier to maintain. Costs were reduced by lowering floor-to-floor heights, reducing the thickness of external walls from 300mm to 250mm, and keeping central cores as small as possible.

The 1.5-kilometre-long site straddles railway tracks going into Blackfriars. Trains were stopped for 17 days, during which time a viaduct was partly dismantled, a bridge removed, the train tracks realigned and a huge raft constructed over the tracks to form the base of the development. All the buildings rest on springs which attenuate the vibrations from the underground trains much more than the usual Neoprene pads, making the movements less jarring and the buildings effectively bouncy. The courtyard between the buildings is occupied by a painted-steel sculpture by Bruce McLean.

This project was an exercise in how to cut building costs and work with fewer staff. There was even a pilot scheme to challenge the ritual of the British workman's tea break. Bovis, the construction managers, encouraged workers to take breaks at flexible times in 'satellite' canteens on site. To avoid a complete shutdown at 9.00 when all the workers went off to the café for breakfast, it was suggested that breakfast be served on site, keeping the employees at work 20 per cent longer each day. This system has since become a common feature (even a requirement) of many large building sites, with a new generation of satellite greasy spoons now in orbit.

Skidmore, Owings & Merrill, Inc. 1992

LUDGATE

INDIVIDUAL BUILDINGS

1 LUDGATE PLACE

Skidmore, Owings & Merrill, Inc. 1992

Steel frame, panelised wall system of steel fins and aluminium spandrels.

10 LUDGATE PLACE

Skidmore, Owings & Merrill, Inc. 1992

Steel frame with unitised system of aluminium and granite fins.

100 LUDGATE HILL

Skidmore, Owings & Merrill, Inc. 1992

Reinforced-concrete structure, precast-concrete panelised system with limestone.

100 NEW BRIDGE STREET

RHWL 1992

Steel frame with precast-concrete cladding.

ADDRESS Ludgate Hill, London EC4

CLIENT Rosehaugh Stanhope Development plc in conjunction with British Rail Property Board

TOTAL CONTRACT VALUE £400 million

SIZE 76,250 square metres

TUBE Blackfriars – Circle, District Lines

ACCESS none

Skidmore, Owings & Merrill, Inc. 1992

BROADGATE

The City of London is the home of a strong international commercial power. During the 1980s, Thatcher's government deregulated many financial activities to open up a new age of international electronic trading. Banks and brokers merged, and started to demand a new type of office with large floorplates, floor-to-floor heights big enough to accommodate underfloor cabling, and spaces that could be flexible, could cope with 24-hour operations and would be suitable for employees working in highly stressful conditions. The demand was met between 1985 and 1991 by the addition of 4.5 million square metres of office space in central London. Broadgate provided some 334,450 square metres of this space, equal to the amount provided by five Empire State Buildings.

The site has for more than a century been a crossover point between the City and the influx of employees arriving at Liverpool Street Station. Globally, it sits between New York and Tokyo, providing a perfect base for foreign financiers.

Extensive research into client requirements revealed that North American office environments were admired: that is, the face of the buildings should be impressive and they should contain big lobbies and atriums, large open-plan office floors, and facilities that would enhance the lives of the employees – outdoor spaces, restaurants, bars and a health club. All these undertakings were achieved at Broadgate within the context of the medieval street plan and listed buildings.

The whole scheme consists of 13 buildings and three squares, built in 14 phases. The first four phases were masterminded by Arup Associates. The plan was generated from the patterns of movement of people coming to the site from Liverpool Street Station. Each phase had to be built in 12 months, taking six years in all. The secret to this speedy building system was the prefabrication of many building parts off site. Most of the buildings have a steel frame with metal deck floors and external cladding to accommodate any-

Arup Associates/Skidmore, Owings & Merrill, Inc. 1984–91

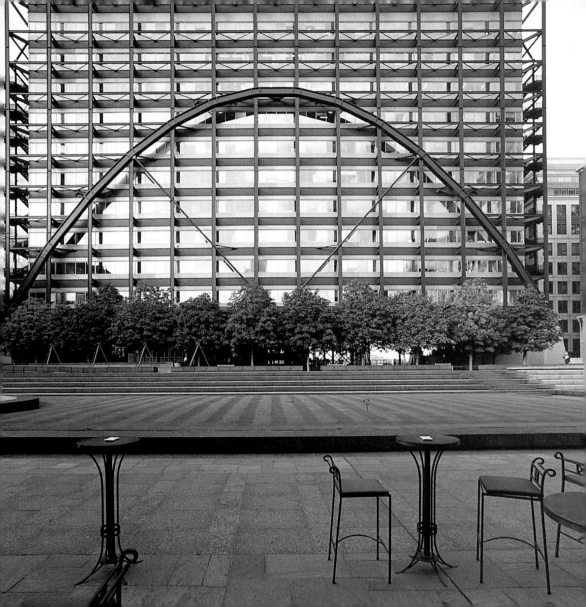

BROADGATE

thing from an auditorium to a trading floor. Complete units, such as toilet pods, lift shafts and plant rooms, and the granite cladding with heating services incorporated, were all prefabricated and slotted into the steel frame.

More than half of the site is built on a raft which spans the railway tracks of Liverpool Street Station. Specific parts of the buildings were made by specialist fabricators under direct contract to the client in order to avoid the administrative mayhem of contractors and sub-contractors. The project involved 2200 people on site and 19,000 drawings per week, so keeping simple and direct lines of communication open was essential.

Of particular interest is Exchange House, by the Chicago firm Skidmore, Owings & Merrill, Inc. This building owes much to bridge technology since its four parabolic arches span the railway tracks. They rest on eight piers which support the entire structure. The steel-framed box that encloses the office floors hangs between the arches. This is the most expressive of all the Broadgate buildings because of the innovative technology used to create the container, articulated in the rawest of materials. The modern exterior hints at the contents of the interior, which is equipped with the most advanced information technology in Britain. The square in front gives a superb, full-length view of the inside of the vaulted train sheds at Liverpool Street Station.

Also notable is Broadgate Square by Arup Associates, with its circular ice rink in the centre surrounded by tiered terraces, like an amphitheatre, with cascading foliage. The terraces accommodate restaurants, bars and shops behind which are the glass and granite façades of the office buildings. The square provides the desired public recreation area, but the surrounding buildings are faceless, making it seem an abrupt transition within the scheme, fully animated only at brief intervals in the day or at certain times of year. People seem to be forced to the place out of necessity rather than being drawn to it.

Arup Associates/Skidmore, Owings & Merrill, Inc. 1984–91

BROADGATE

Helping to redeem the generally feeble architecture are the contributions by many well-known contemporary artists who were commissioned to make work especially for the site. The vast steel sheets that make up *Fulcrum* by Richard Serra rest tentatively against each other at the entrance to Broadgate Square, forming an integral part of the landscape. *Leaping Hare on Crescent and Bell* by Barry Flanagan sits in the square. The work inside 100 Liverpool Street includes a bronze horse by Flanagan, a terrazzo reception desk and mural by Bruce McLean, and prints by Patrick Caulfield.

ADDRESS Broadgate, London EC2

CLIENT Rosehaugh Stanhope Development plc in conjunction with British Rail Property Board

CONSTRUCTION MANAGEMENT Bovis & Schal

SIZE 3.6 hectares

TUBE Liverpool Street – Central, Circle, Hammersmith & City, Metropolitan Lines

ACCESS public spaces are open

THE CITY

Arup Associates/Skidmore, Owings & Merrill, Inc. 1984–91

NORTH AND EAST LONDON

CULLINAN / HARBOUR HOUSES

1998 saw the tenth anniversary of the purchase of this site by two young architects who were designing office blocks in conventional practices at the time (hence their familiarity with concrete for the primary structure). Ivan Harbour is now an associate at the Richard Rogers Partnership; Dominic Cullinan was working in Ian Ritchie's office but has since set up his own practice. Ten years later the building is by no means finished.

From the outset the intention was to build a home for each partner and to build it themselves as cashflow permitted. The initial plan envisaged a house at the front of the site and one at the rear backing on to a parking lot, but the buildings would have been too close for facing properties. Today two four-storey homes sit side by side facing the street, with a garden at the rear and a glorified garden shed, backing on to the parking lot, which has functioned as everything from home to Cullinan and family to kitchen for Harbour and family while they install a permanent kitchen facility in their house.

The two houses grow outwards from a stairwell that provides a shared structural core for the whole building. This core is leaf-shaped in plan and takes the double helix of a DNA strand as its form, so the space left behind by one spiral is occupied by another winding in the opposite direction. For a grand comparison, the stair tower at the Chateau de Blois (1508), attributed to Leonardo da Vinci, performs a similar function. A more utilitarian example is the fire-escape stairs inserted in many US office blocks. The double strand uses space efficiently while maintaining separate means of access.

The plan of each house is long and narrow and they are naturally lit through full-height glazing on the front and rear elevations. The narrow plan is compensated by generous floor-to-ceiling heights, with the first floor cut away at the rear to create a double-height space on the ground floor. The stairs emerge at the top of each house into a crow's-nest room then continue on to a roof terrace, creating a lightwell over the stair.

Dominic Cullinan and Ivan Harbour 1988–

CULLINAN/HARBOUR HOUSES

Windows on the front elevation are lined in an opaque corrugated plastic that both insulates and obscures direct views into the houses.

Harbour describes the project as 'evolutionary' rather than 'revolutionary', and the building has come about by purely organic means (it took six months to make the formwork for each section of the stair core and one hour to pour it, hence each pour was a different experience).The building team comprised juniors at Ove Arup & Partners who tried out their engineering skills (there is more concrete below ground than above), several generations of students from the Architectural Association and willing family members. The same limited budget encouraged the acquisition of a magpie's nest of left-over materials collected from building merchants and sites.

The Hackney Society wants to list the houses as one of its significant buildings of the twentieth century – perhaps the first time an unfinished building has been deemed worthy of such reverence. An inspiration to any would-be self-builder.

NORTH AND EAST LONDON

ADDRESS 1 Trumans Road, London N16
STRUCTURAL ENGINEER ongoing advice from participating employees of Arup
SIZE 260-square-metre site
RAIL Dalston Kingsland
ACCESS contact Dominic Cullinan Architecture on 020 7923 7100

Dominic Cullinan and Ivan Harbour 1988–

BRADBURY STREET COMMUNITY WORKSHOPS/MARKET STALLS

Dalston: home of the fantastic Ridley Road Market, the Kingsland Waste Market on Saturday, of Turkish grocery stores, African nightclubs, cheap cigarette sellers and of unprecedented financial hardship; not so long ago it was the cheapest place to buy food in south-east England. Unlike Hackney to the east, grappling with its unwieldy council estates, much of Dalston is no more than the three-storey height of its run-down Victorian terrace housing stock. And unlike Stoke Newington to the north, centred on Clissold Park, Dalston does not exude the village atmosphere attractive to so many young professionals and their fledgling families.

Dalston is currently host to a diverse range of initiatives aimed at helping the existing population to thrive and to provide opportunities for local skills and marginal businesses to secure a foothold in the area. The Peabody Trust has committed homes to the here (see pages 246–250), the planned East London Underground line will link the area directly with the City (eventually) and the Bradbury Street Workshops by their very usefulness seek to reintroduce a feeling of safety in 'a "no-go" late night area'.

This two-phase urban design project was developed over a period of five years by local community developers, Hackney Co-operative Developments, architect Russell Brown (director of Hawkins\Brown) and existing and potential tenants, as part of a long-term scheme aimed at the transformation of the whole of Dalston. The first phase created a series of workshops and shops in a rebuilt Victorian terrace with communal access provided at first- and second-floor levels at the rear of the terrace overlooking the car park. A new rotunda building at the end of the row provides shared meeting rooms with a bar on the ground floor. It faces both the street and the car park and therefore acts as the beacon for the project.

The second phase incorporated the permanent and lockable market stalls for small

Hawkins\Brown 1999

BRADBURY STREET COMMUNITY WORKSHOPS/MARKET STALLS

businesses at ground-floor level facing the car park. Materials are robust and simply detailed – the market stalls were constructed off-site.

The intervention does not draw attention to itself as architectural do-goodery but rather leaves room for its most important architectural achievement; a scheme without edges and boundaries which allows for future expansion and partnership with other schemes. Words like 'regeneration' and 'sustainability' feature largely in the architectural vocabulary and are used all too loosely and inaccurately by architects and journalists alike. From fund-raising strategy to method of procurment, this project proves an inspiring exception.

ADDRESS Bradbury Street, London N16
CLIENT Hackney Co-operative Development
ENGINEER Price & Myers
RAIL Dalston Kingsland
ACCESS open

Hawkins\Brown 1999

TWENTIETH-CENTURY WING
GEFFRYE MUSEUM

The Geffrye Museum – formerly the almshouses of the Worshipful Company of Ironmongers (built 1715) and now Grade-I listed – specialises in the furniture and domestic interiors of the urban middle classes, with period rooms laid out in sequence from 1600 to 1900. In 1990 an additional wing was planned to bring the displays up to the present day. One of the first and largest buildings to be awarded funds from the lottery, the new wing houses the twentieth-century rooms, a new restaurant and shop, a gallery space for temporary displays, a design centre for work by local craftsmen, a store for items not on display, and two education studios. The design process was closely monitored by English Heritage and the Hackney Society, both of whom were keen to see the new wing as a building in its own right without attempting to ape the Queen Anne style of the almshouses. The main concerns were the way the old and new would meet and that any new structure would not impose on the symmetry of the existing buildings.

On entering the main gates of the museum there is no evidence of the new extension. The land falling away at the south-eastern corner behind the main buildings accommodates a two-storey construction by sinking the lower floor into the ground. The new site protrudes into the urban landscape of a disused railway line, a late 1980s office development and the backs of houses, and it was the challenge of pulling together these incongruous parts to create some kind of urban unity that excited the architects and resulted in this long, bendy, brick and timber-raftered shed with a slate roof. The horseshoe-shaped plan enables the continuation of the linear progression of displays while fitting into a smaller site.

The glass-wrapped transitional space between the eighteenth-century right-angled walls of the former almshouses and Branson Coates' obliquely angled spaces forms a semi-outdoor room for a restaurant and shop. Key elements are picked out and expressed

Branson Coates Architecture 1998

TWENTIETH-CENTURY WING, GEFFRYE MUSEUM

as sculptural gestures to re-emphasise the distinction between old and new and to clarify a logical means of circulation within the new building: a suspended ceiling made on a dia-grid pattern floats through the common areas, helping to direct visitors through the space. The gently contoured surface draws the eye down the middle of the plan to the permanent displays around the windowless curved back of the building. The ceiling is suspended in such a way as to provide clerestory lighting to the central space, above a cast-concrete spiral stair with a scaly glass balustrade and copper rainwater pipes forming the central pillar which leads to the ancillary facilities at semi-basement level. A sloped ha-ha dug around the base of the building allows daylight to penetrate the lower level.

The use of traditional materials and the modelling of the interior spaces reflect the scale and intimacy of the eighteenth-century buildings while twisting their original meaning: exterior brick walls are built on sloping courses in a continuous curve creating the illusory effect of a Möbius strip, though all walls are built with lime mortar and without expansion joints in the traditional way. The new wing is absolutely the 'sympathetic partner with a spirit of its own' that Nigel Coates first envisaged.

ADDRESS Kingsland Road, London E2
STRUCTURAL ENGINEER Alan Baxter Associates
CONTRACT VALUE £5.3 million
SIZE 1900 square metres
TUBE Liverpool Street – Central, Circle, Hammersmith & City, Metropolitan Lines/Old Street – Northern Line
ACCESS open Tuesday to Saturday, 10.00–17.00; Sunday, 14.00–17.00

Branson Coates Architecture 1998

S GREER

Handbag designer S Greer required a gallery, shop (their first) and working area in a room that measures no more than 5 by 5 metres. One's first thought would perhaps not be to fill an already confined space with an enormous piece of furniture. Yet this is exactly what the young WaG architects have done. The strategy has worked absolutely to their advantage, for when you call the piece of furniture a 'Vertical Landscape' (it is indeed made up of contoured layers of white painted MDF to create a model-glacier-like chunk) and cover the entire end wall in mirrored glass, this shoebox becomes a marvelously endless-scape of clouds or snow or 3-D computer imagining, wherever you prefers to locate yourself. The architects describe it thus: 'the topological patterning … is generated through the interference of three rhythmic orders. These orders, and their frequencies, were determined by the commodity range and the consumer's visual and tactile field.'

The 'object' is the shop; contours form shelves and sections pull out seamlessly to create larger table surfaces for counter space. Horizontal strips of mirror are applied to the left-hand wall, with white gallery-wall space between. Workspace is housed inside the right-hand wall behind and between flush cupboards. WaG Architecture have designed their way through a very small space rather than out of one, creating a thoroughly worthwhile detour from Bond Street.

ADDRESS 37a Retford Street (opposite Café 122 on Kingsland Road), London N1
CLIENT Sally Greer
SIZE 20 square metres
TUBE Old Street – Northern Line
ACCESS by appointment; www.sallygreer.com

WaG Architecture 2002

HACKNEY COMMUNITY COLLEGE

This is one of the largest new further-education campuses in the UK, running vocational courses, adult- and community-education classes and a Sixth Form Centre. These courses were formerly provided through 13 college centres and more than 80 outreach venues throughout the borough. The new Shoreditch Campus houses two-thirds of the college (14,000 full- and part-time students), a public library and a one-stop shop for the council.

The key elements of the design were developed by Sir Colin Stansfield-Smith of Hampshire County Architects, the godfather of that county's outstanding primary-school programme. The central theme of many of the Hampshire schools was the creation of a micro-habitat centred on a communal space to which other areas have direct access. The Shoreditch Campus focuses on two large courtyards, one of which is bisected by two three-storey Edwardian school buildings refurbished by Hawkins\Brown.

The design concept of standardised three-storey blocks linked by vertical service cores is well suited to phased construction and flexibility. The blocks have concrete frames clad in buff brickwork and high-performance aluminium-framed glazing, with pitched roofs made of glue-laminated timber beams and insulated metal cladding.

In order that the primary north (Falkirk Street) and west (Hoxton Street) boundary walls did not read as battlements from the outside, a series of artist-designed gates and screens has been incorporated into the brickwork. These provide views into the campus and maintain a sense of scale with the surrounding streets. Retained Edwardian school buildings provide a context that enriches the much larger areas of new building.

The main entrance on Falkirk Street is at the corner of the north courtyard: a large, hard-landscaped area surrounded on three sides by three-storey blocks. The Learning Resource Centre is in the middle of the courtyard at semi-basement level and connects underground to the library. The centre is approached via a sunken amphitheatre on one side

Hampshire County Architects/Percy Ogden Architects 1997–2001

and is flanked on the other by a water feature bordered by a 2-metre-long blue wall designed by Susanna Heron (other artworks include the benches around the amphitheatre by Bettina Furnee, a ceramic fountain by Lotte Glob, gates by Matthew Fedden and stone seats in the south courtyard by Pat Kaufman). Two shallow, glazed protrusions emerging from the landscaped roof of the centre allow light into the subterranean room. The smaller south courtyard is soft-landscaped and is dominated by the two Edwardian buildings.

The main circulation routes are a key feature of the internal courtyards. The routes are defined by perimeter colonnades formed from a skeletal hardwood structure that reaches to the full height of the buildings. The structure also accommodates high-level sun louvres and lower-level membrane canopies to provide shelter from the rain.

Much of the success of the project can be attributed to the decisions of the college directors to involve local people from the outset and to appoint their own project managers from within the college. Hackney has some of the highest rates of poverty and poor housing in Britain, the highest rate of unemployment of any London borough, and 33.6 per cent of its population is made up of minority ethnic groups, the majority of whom do not speak English as their first language. If any London neighbourhood needs a facility of this quality it is this one – and it should serve as a solid model for councils to adopt. Better still, make it a standard national requirement.

ADDRESS Shoreditch Campus, Falkirk Street, London N1
STRUCTURAL ENGINEER Buro Happold Consulting Engineers/Whitby Bird& Partners
CONTRACT VALUE approximately £40 million
TUBE Old Street – Northern Line
ACCESS by appointment only – enquiries to Jacqui Hurst on 020 7613 9125/9034

Hampshire County Architects/Percy Ogden Architects 1997–2001

PEABODY TRUST HOUSING

The Peabody Trust was established by American philanthropist George Peabody in 1862 in order to 'ameliorate the condition of the poor and needy of this great metropolis and to promote their comfort and happiness'. The first development (1862–64) was designed by H A Darbishire in Commercial Street, E1. Today the Trust owns 19,000 rentable homes and is one of London's leading regeneration agencies. The majority of its properties are well-maintained, austere Victorian brick blocks. However, it has recently taken an innovative approach, employing new technologies to push down construction costs and maximising the energy efficiency of buildings to bring savings to tenants. Soaring land prices have coincided with a long-term shortage of skilled labour, raising the cost of traditional building above the range of social-housing providers. In response the Trust recognises that it needs to develop new techniques and provide a mixture of uses. Three of the most recent developments include modular housing in Murray Grove, housing and commercial space in Dalston Lane, and homes and workshops in Westferry Road.

MURRAY GROVE, designed by Cartwright Pickard, was built in just seven months in 1998. Thirty modular homes (the first of their kind in Britain) comprise prefabricated steel units equipped with all plumbing, electrics, doors, windows, bathroom and kitchen fittings, tiles and carpets. Each one measures 8 by 3.2 by 3 metres to fit on the back of an articulated lorry for transport between factory and site. The units are a monocoque structure so that each can sit on top of another without a separate structural frame. Access decks and balconies clip on to the modules. While this prototype cost more than traditional construction, the benefits lie in future economies of scale and enduring quality.

DALSTON LANE was designed in 2000 by Allford Hall Monaghan Morris. The scheme provides 24 flats for rent (at below market rates) over three floors in a single horizontal block. Six commercial units project forward from the block at street level; a court-

various architects 1998–2003

yard provides parking space and servicing areas. Bedrooms face north on to Dalston Lane; the high-ceilinged main living and eating spaces face south through a glazed elevation with mesh balconies attached. Access to the flats is through folds in the blue glazed-brick flanking walls at either end of the block. The chequer-board pattern of the upper level façades is not as arbitrary as Sir Edwin Lutyens' famous 1928 chequered housing blocks in Victoria. Here they are rendered and painted (with a 1970s-social-housing-in-the-Eastern-block palette) according to the grid of expansion joints.

WESTFERRY ROAD was designed by CZWG. It is located at the confluence of two major transport networks – the Docklands Light Railway on the north side and Westferry Road to the east. The development provides commercial premises on the ground floor and three floors above of live/work studios in three building blocks made from load-bearing brick with steel and concrete floors. The design adopts a traditional light-industrial plan around a central courtyard which creates a focus for the activities of the building: access/arrival/departure. The blocks are united by a common perimeter wall, which in true CZWG style vies for attention in this fast-lane site (a normal street sign would go unnoticed here) through the use of 9-metre-high letters integrated into the brickwork.

Continuing its development of off-site construction techniques to maximise quality and cost-effectiveness in new-build housing schemes, the Peabody Trust (under the inscrutable guidance of its chief commissioning architect, Dickon Robinson) continues to scrutinise and exploit the possibilities of modular/prefabricated construction.

RAINES DAIRY, also designed by Allford Hall Monaghan Morris and completed in 2003, comprises 61 homes (for rent) arranged within three blocks linked in a T-shape by a central circulation core. Eight live/work units (for outright sale) form the Northwold Road frontage at street level with two-bedroom homes on the upper four floors. Three-bedroom

various architects 1998–2003

PEABODY TRUST HOUSING

family homes are located at the rear of the site overlooking gardens and parking space. Yorkon Ltd has provided fully fitted-out modules with bathrooms, kitchens, tiling, wardrobes, lighting heating, plumbing, balconies and balustrading. Cladding is applied subsequently although the architects have worked to include this in the complete package for future projects. Roof elements, staircases and access decks also come as prefabricated elements – each one is craned into position as at Murray Grove.

The procurement of the project was conducted using the innovative P.P.C 2000 form of contract. This contract looks to the client, contractors and design team to sign up to a programme of meetings to discuss key issues with the aim of reducing disputes at all levels of the project, from optimising off-site construction and reducing on-site trades, thus minimising the extent of snagging on completion, to reducing the length of the construction period, lowering overall costs. With so much 'reduction' on the agenda the architects have managed (by market standards) to maximise the space in each home by creating open-plan living/kitchen rooms and incorporating front and rear balconies to each floor, reinforcing the benefits of new-build schemes in facilitating modern living standards.

For details of more Peabody Trust developments, call its press office on 020 7922 0202.

ADDRESSES Murray Grove, London N1 (Old Street – Northern Line)/Dalston Lane, London E8 (Dalston Kingsland – rail)/Westferry Road, London E14 (Westferry – DLR)/ Raines Dairy, Northwold Road, London N16 (Stoke Newington – rail)
ACCESS none to individual homes

various architects 1998–2003

HOUSE AND OFFICE

'America is the original version of modernity ... America ducks the question of origins; it cultivates no origin or mythical authenticity; it has no past and no founding truth. Having known no primitive accumulation of time, it lives in a perpetual present ... it lives in perpetual simulation, in a perpetual present of signs.' Jean Baudrillard, *America* (Verso 1988)

Anyone who thought postmodernism was a late-20th-century concept pioneered in the US will be surprised to find that it has sprouted new shoots this side of the millennium in Hackney, East London. This building, a townhouse incorporating office space and a flat for rent, represents one of those 'signs' that Baudrillard referred to. Like a suburban graffito, the combination of naïve iconography and traditional construction method (cavity walls clad in imitation wood cement fibreboard painted sky blue) collaborates with a politically idealistic view of the regeneration of run-down inner-city neighbourhoods; a 1950s representation of the home and work bound defensively into the confines of a gritty site, like a promotional visit by Doris Day to an industrial estate. 'The design evolved out of an earlier competition entry for a billboard house whose premise was that the front façade would house advertising posters which would help pay for its construction'.

If, as FAT state, architecture's future is 'as information for living', this is the cartoon on the editorial page, the purpose of which is not always to make readers smile.

ADDRESS 2a Garner Street, London E2
CLIENT Sean Griffiths
ENGINEER Elliott Wood Partnership
TUBE Bethnal Green – Central Line **RAIL** Cambridge Heath
ACCESS restricted – this is a private house

FAT 2002

THE HOTHOUSE

The new offices of the Free Form Arts Trust are in the heart of an area of urban and community regeneration; near to the refurbishment of the Hackney Empire, a Technology and Learning Centre and the major Ocean music venue. The Hothouse project forms a link between this new 'Cultural Quarter' in one of London's poorest boroughs and the area's open spaces.

The Hothouse is located at the corner of London Fields alongside the elevated mainline railway. It provides office and studio spaces, training facilities and a conference space in one building and live/work units for artists in refurbished railway arches. Boomerang-shaped in plan, the building follows the corner of the park boundary and defines the edge of a courtyard area between itself and the arches. On the park side amoeboid window openings will catch glimpses of the park itself (the building's occupants are waiting for planting to mature before dismantling hoardings). The railway side has a large expanse of glazing with brick panels and gridded projections as protection from noise and vibration.

Working with a large group of clients in a fluid hierarchy while managing the expectations of the community and planners sounds like the context of all built projects, but here there is a mutual understanding that the design has to provide a changing set of scenarios rather than a fixed model. A common vocabulary has been invented around the project, to be used as a resource for future development in and around the site.

ADDRESS east side of London Fields, London E8
STRUCTURAL ENGINEER Dewhurst Macfarlane & Partners
M&E ENGINEER Michael Popper Associates
RAIL London Fields
ACCESS open 9.30–17.30; visit by appointment (telephone 020 7249 3394)

Ash Sakula Architects 2002

ABBEY MILLS PUMPING STATION

The above-ground enclosure used less than 7 per cent of the overall budget. Much of the major engineering project lies underground inside a reinforced-concrete substructure incorporating new low-level culverts which pump sewage to be discharged at a higher level. Pumping equipment is at ground-floor level with a central spine at first-floor level for the generators and switchgear. Air intakes and extracts protrude from this central spine and through the roof on either side.

The extruded section is shaped by the substructure and provides a smooth bubble of gleaming metal cladding around the superstructure. Steel portal frames form side aisles which support catwalks for equipment maintenance. The central spine is made up of similar portal frames with bow-string roof beams spanning between inner and outer portals.

The deep pitch of the roof allows the building to lie low in a landscape that is to be converted into meadowland. The pumping station's precursor (1865–68) stands adjacent to the site (retained for storm pumping) – an outstanding example of Victorian engineering by Joseph Bazalgette that uses Moorish, Byzantine and Gothic features to disguise its identity. Allies & Morrison allude to these references in the shape of their roof, but they express the function of the building through a scale and materials.

ADDRESS Abbey Lane, London E15
STRUCTURAL ENGINEERS superstructure Ove Arup & Partners/substructure Trafalgar House Technology
CONTRACT VALUE enclosure £2 million/whole project £30 million
TUBE Bromley-by-Bow – District Line
ACCESS none

Allies & Morrison 1997

SWANLEA SECONDARY SCHOOL

This, the first new secondary school to be built in London after a ten-year hiatus, is designed to accommodate 1050 pupils, with meeting rooms for use outside school hours. More significantly, the layout and size of the classrooms and communication between them have been informed by the demands of the National Curriculum, making it the first school of its kind. It provides a new focus and social centre for a community which is culturally rich but economically run-down.

The plan focuses on a central covered street or mall, lined by brick buildings which in turn surround a series of courtyards and gardens on the south side and a car park on the north. The dramatic sweep of the glass mall roof greets you on Brady Street and draws you into the heart of the scheme: an avenue flanked by curved, tapered columns restrained by clusters of diagonal struts which support the glazing. During winter the mall acts as a heat source for the whole scheme. The roof is made from a specialised glass made up of prismatic strips that reflect the high summer sun and let in low winter sun. During the summer the mall is ventilated at a high level, creating cross-ventilation vertically through the space. Classrooms have shop windows fronting the mall so that work can be presented to the school community and to make maximum use of natural light, heat and ventilation.

The gardens are outdoor classrooms: one is an ecological garden, another an exhibition courtyard. Eerily marking the south-west corner of the site is the caretaker's house, a stop-off point on the Jack the Ripper bus tour.

ADDRESS Brady Street, London E1
CONTRACT VALUE £9.2 million **SIZE** 10,500 square metres
TUBE Whitechapel – District, Hammersmith & City Lines
ACCESS restricted

Percy Thomas Partnership/Hampshire County Architects 1991–93

STRATFORD MARKET DEPOT

Having failed to win the bid for the Jubilee Line Extension station at London Bridge, Chris Wilkinson Architects did well to win its first major commission here at Stratford instead. An outline scheme, fee bid and management proposal for a train shed (for the inspection and maintenance of 11 trains), control building (to survey a secure area for 33 trains adjacent to the main shed), workshops and stores, offices and amenities and a traction sub-station were compiled in two weeks, with the finished building remaining remarkably true to the early plans.

The site was determined by the archeological remains of a medieval abbey found to its east and the layout of the existing tracks. Safety requires that tracks straighten out before entering a building, thus determining the 30-degree cut-off angle of the front entrance and the consequent parallelogram plan. All administrative and amenities buildings are lined up regimentally in grey uniforms along the west side of the main shed, each unit designed to suit its function while using common construction details.

The train-shed roof is a 100-metre-long, gently curving span with clear headroom of 8 metres above the tracks. The roof structure is a space frame formed on a diagrid rather than on a conventional orthogonal grid because of the angles produced by the parallelogram plan. Two rows of columns form divisions between the three categories of internal operations in the building, thus enabling the overall roof span to be reduced. Each concrete-filled steel column extends into three branched arms to carry the load and meet the space frame at regular intervals. The V-shaped pattern of the columns on the long elevations provides lateral stability while the tracery created by the columns and space frame, painted white and pale green respectively, enhances the lightness of the vast structure. Daylight is admitted from all sides of the building: through the roof (striated with openable rooflights), the south wall (clad in translucent fibreglass), clerestory glazing in the

Chris Wilkinson Architects 1997

STRATFORD MARKET DEPOT

side walls, and the north wall, which is made of a special suspended-glass system pur-pose-designed in conjunction with Pilkington.

One of the client's conditions was that the architect and structural engineer should have equal rights as lead consultants, to build a co-operative relationship from the out-set. The building demonstrates the effectiveness of this way of working, with neither party attempting to gain ground over the other by obscuring aspects of the design process or adding unnecessary elements for effect. As with all good industrial buildings, the Stratford Market Depot and its ancillary structures are unhampered by the daunting lack of context and stand out as pure expressions of function, structure and materials.

NORTH AND EAST LONDON

ADDRESS Angel Lane, London e15
CLIENT London Underground
STRUCTURAL ENGINEER Hyder Consulting
CONTRACT VALUE approximately £18 million
SIZE 11-hectare site (main shed 19,000 square metres)
TUBE Stratford – Central Line
ACCESS very restricted

Chris Wilkinson Architects 1997

STRATFORD BUS STATION

Like a tent in the desert, the bus-station canopy is a welcome retreat from the jammed one-way system that strangles a desolate suburban borough centre. It is the first in a series of new transport buildings planned for East London alongside the extension of the Jubilee Line (see page 326) and additions to the Docklands Light Railway (see page 298). The roof canopy rises gracefully above the bedlam. It is made up of tensile-fabric inverted umbrellas supported by a forest of steel columns set out on a grid to define the main waiting area. Each column contains channels for roof drainage and cable conduit for lighting. The inverted-canopy form allows double-decker buses to draw up to the stop beneath the shelter. Concourse services are encased in building blocks around the perimeter of the sheltered area and clad in graffiti-proof glass panels.

Despite clear sightlines throughout the concourse, the absence of blind corners and enclosed spaces and the generous glazed screens shielding the waiting rooms, the structure is still draped in an assortment of security paraphernalia such as video monitors and loudspeakers.

ADDRESS Great Eastern Road, London E15

CLIENT London Transport Buses

IN-HOUSE ARCHITECT Soji Abass

STRUCTURAL ENGINEER Anthony Hunt Associates

CONTRACT VALUE £2 million

DOCKLANDS LIGHT RAILWAY Stratford

TUBE Stratford – Central Line

ACCESS open

London Bus Transport Passenger Infrastructure 1994

THE GREEN BRIDGE

The concept behind The Green Bridge is that Mile End Park should win over the thundering traffic of the Mile End Road. The idea of joining the two halves of Mile End Park with a piece of landscape was a key gesture in the regeneration proposals for the park overall. The compilation of urban fragments that make up the surrounding area is united by this bold and beautiful feature resting on new retail units at street level (the revenue from these lettings contributing substantially to park maintenance).

The bridge is 25 metres wide with a 6-metre-wide cycle route and pathway in the middle, and planting on either side. Railings are set back 2 metres from the edges to prevent anyonedropping things on to the road below. To avoid a tunnel effect beneath, the yellow soffit of the bridge has been designed as a curved surface sloping up towards the edges, reducing the impact of the width of the bridge over the retail spaces. Landscaping of the bridge deck is a continuation of the park itself.

The completion of this new piece of park marks a big step away from the acceptance of a lowest common denominator. What might simply have been a footbridge is transformed into a floating garden and catalyst for new planting and imaginative landscaping elsewhere in the park. A school overlooks the site and now uses it as an outdoor classroom, bringing new meaning to a phrase directed at delinquent children – 'go play on the traffic interchange'.

ADDRESS Mile End Park, London E3 (corner of Mile End Road and Grove Road)
CLIENT London Borough of Tower Hamlets
CONTRACT VALUE £5.8 million
TUBE Mile End – Central and District Lines
ACCESS open

CZWG Architects 2000

PLASHET SCHOOL BRIDGE

On seeing the bridge, an American critic wondered how any client could ever be convinced that they should want such a thing … but was jolly glad that they had. The school required some sort of covered link between two buildings that sit on opposite sides of a busy road with students having to travel between them frequently during the day. A brutish scheme was devised by the borough's engineers, and promptly refused by the planners. The architects were subsequently invited to 'decorate a bridge'. And so the scheme developed, from mere decoration to a building in its own right.

The bridge connects the main school campus with a seriously tough yet eminently distinguished 1960s teaching block by Whitby & McMorran. Because of the different alignment of the two buildings and the mature trees en route, the bridge was designed with a curve. The concept was to create a journey with a meeting place in the middle. Emphasising the central junction as an expressive feature allowed the architects to disguise a complex connection where the geometry of the two sides of the bridge meet but do not match.

With so few components to make up the bridge, many have dual functions. These features are primarily to deal with the issue of rainwater drainage and as a result the structure is alive with gutters and funnels and channels. The bridge is constructed with the largest standard size carriage beams available (915 mm) which also act as balustrades. The handrail doubles up as a drainage pipe. Steel sheet spans between the lower flanges to form the platform and torsional restraint. A Teflon-coated fabric roof is stretched between asymmetrical steel hoops bolted to the beams. These hoops accommodate lighting, while gutters are sewn into the fabric sections. Small steel funnels connect between the gutters and the handrail drainpipe which in turn carries rainwater down the folded edge of the 32mm plate-steel piers which support the bridge.

Bird Portchmouth Russum 2000

PLASHET SCHOOL BRIDGE

A walk through the bridge is a heightened sensory experience; it is noisy, cold in winter, its insides more intestinal than interior as light catches the swollen fabric undulations, altering one's perception of the space with every step. The plate-steel work and mechanical drainage system is of a scale and texture more akin to submarine construction than pedestrian walkway – at its most successful in the cut and folded piers. In my mind the central meeting point feature is inconsistent with the rest of the bridge by not being expressive enough. The sheets of steel that slice the bridge in two and the plate-steel piers appear to have been drawn by a different hand.

The whole structure was assembled during the six-week summer holiday with the actual lifting of the bridge sections carried out over a weekend. The bridge is boldly individual – the sort of impression that a school would wish to make.

ADDRESS Plashet Grove, London E6
CLIENT Education Department of the London Borough of Newham
STRUCTURAL ENGINEER Techniker
CONTRACT VALUE £550,000
SIZE 67 metres long
TUBE East Ham – District Line
ACCESS inside by permission only

Bird Portchmouth Russum 2000

DOCKLANDS AND THE GREENWICH PENINSULA

CONTROL CENTRE AND LIFTING BRIDGES

In the shadow of the monstrous Canary Wharf development, the gleaming Control Centre has invented an unselfconscious architecture all of its own. Starting with the design intention of revealing all the bridges' working parts, the architects have ingeniously created a separate building to house the hydraulic plant required to operate the counterweight system of the lifting bridges.

The simple steel-frame and steel-panel construction (welded on site) has been stretched and details exaggerated to create a bold, sculptural form. Each feature – gutter, air vents, staircase and control cabin – is an integral part of the structure, not a decorative afterthought. The great A-frames, pivots and hydraulic rams are now in full view, as are the mooring platform, fishing platform and public staircase – all dramatic silver elements set against the primary white structure of the bridges.

Many of these bascule bridges can be found in and around Chicago. This one, however, remains symbolic rather than practical as at present ocean liners do not navigate these docks.

ADDRESS Canary Wharf, Eastern Access, London E14
CLIENT London Docklands Development Corporation
ENGINEER Mott MacDonald Civil Ltd
COST £4 million
DOCKLANDS LIGHT RAILWAY Canary Wharf
ACCESS none

Alsop Lyall & Störmer 1990

CASCADES

Twenty storeys high, with water on two sides, Cascades holds its head up defiantly in the middle of low-lying Docklands. From a distance the block seems to be a formidable solid lump with an unusual leaning profile, but close up it becomes multi-faceted, made up of layers of windows, balconies, turrets and portholes. The texture of the façades is a result of the plan. A spinal corridor runs through the centre, to either side of which are one-, two- and three-bedroom flats set at angles to capture interesting views and light. The flats have deep, open plans with small cabin bedrooms tucked at the back (nearest the corridor). The sloping side is the fire-escape stair accommodated in a long, shed-shaped enclosure (like a greenhouse) with roof terraces at each side. The view is spectacular. Facilities include a swimming pool (at the bottom of the slope), gymnasium, conference room and some shops.

Cascades has been described as 'a castle for men and women of the right stuff', the types who people Tom Wolfe's novel *Bonfire of the Vanities*. The block is a symbol of the 1980s boom in finance and property, when young professionals came to settle here attracted by the proximity of the City and what seemed a good investment given Canary Wharf rising nearby. With the addition of the Jubilee Line Extension and the current '80s pop-music revival, the development has taken on a new romantic status.

ADDRESS West Ferry Road, London E14
CLIENT Kentish Homes
CONTRACT VALUE £18.8 million
SIZE 164 flats
DOCKLANDS LIGHT RAILWAY South Quay
ACCESS none

CZWG Architects 1986–88

CANARY WHARF

The late Francis Tibbalds, writing in *The Architects' Journal* (7 November 1990), nicely summed up Europe's largest single development:

> If you want to see what, left to its own devices, the private sector produces, one need look no further than the Isle of Dogs, London's Docklands. The British Government's flagship of 'enterprise culture development' and the urban design challenge of the century adds up to little more than market-led, opportunistic chaos – an architectural circus – with a sprinkling of Post-Modern gimmicks, frenzied construction of the megalumps of Canary Wharf and a fairground train to get you there. It is a disappointment to those who live and work there. Sadly, there was a necessary intermediate step between balance sheet and building that got missed in the rush. It is called urban design.

Canary Wharf, excavated in the 1880s, is part of the Isle of Dogs. The warehouses then were the largest in Europe, some up to a thousand metres long. The port was abandoned at the beginning of the 1980s. At the same time, Thatcher's government set up the Urban Development Corporation to regenerate inner cities and to bring together the interests of business and property developers. The Isle of Dogs was declared an 'Enterprise Zone', to be monitored by the London Docklands Development Corporation. Emphasis shifted from creating places that would be accessible and would serve the public to market-led priorities: buildings for particular types of people, and especially for international business.

Canary Wharf was conceived as Britain's new financial centre and one of the three major financial centres of the world, alongside New York and Tokyo. It was believed that the City's older buildings would not be able to cope with the demands of computerisation and a growing business population. The development initially suffered from poor trans-

Skidmore, Owings & Merrill, Inc. (masterplanners) 1988–2000

port links, but with the completion of the Limehouse Link Tunnel and, even more significantly, the Jubilee Line Extension, there is now a direct route by car from the City following the line of the river, and, by Underground from the city centre in 20 minutes. Canary Wharf can at last occupy its intended strategic position in the east of London.

The site is long and thin with buildings of about 14 storeys high around a central square. The plan claims to incorporate the street patterns of London's Regency squares but there is little in either its scale or proportion to substantiate this. The buildings are more 1930s Chicago in scale (and most of the architects involved in the project are American firms).

The landmark is the Canary Wharf Tower by Cesar Pelli. He describes it as: 'a square prism with pyramidal top in the traditional form of the obelisk, which is the most archetypal way of creating a vertical architectural sign ... this is the essence of the skyscraper'. It is the first skyscraper to be clad in stainless steel. Pelli used the material to symbolise the high-tech nature of the activities inside and to reflect light falling on the building. He would have preferred the tower to be taller and more slender, but the LDDC had already laid down rigid sizes for floor plans and heights. Five floors were consequently sliced off the top in order not to obstruct a nearby flight path.

The architects employed on the first phase of Canary Wharf were essentially required to design façades for speculative office blocks, the size and shape of which had been predetermined, so the challenge for each one was to produce a sufficiently bland frontage to suit any occupant. The elevations and the interiors have separate logics. The result is variations on a theme: an international style of classical colonnades, single windows rather than bands of glass, and stripes of stone cladding.

It is more than ten years since this first phase of development was completed. Its

programme was to develop from the inside rather than evolve as a streetscape (this remains in the realm of the public artwork). In this respect it has morphed under the ground into a large shopping mall (at plaza level) providing necessary services for its working population. However, its skyline is also beginning to change with the addition of three new skyscrapers – the Hongkong & Shanghai Banking Corporation's (HSBC) UK Headquarters and Citibank Headquarters, both designed by Foster and Partners, and a speculative tower by Cesar Pelli.

The HSBC headquarters in Hong Kong was acclaimed as one of the architectural landmarks of the 1980s, groundbreaking in many ways from its main structure to the treatment of its services; architectural haute couture. The HSBC UK Headquarters tower is currently under construction with an anticipated completion date of 2001. As it emerges it seems that it will challenge the city's conception of what is fast becoming London's first cluster of skyscrapers, more than the art of architecture. To continue the analogy with the fashion world, this is Foster's diffusion range. Canary Wharf Tower, the leader of the pack, is now vying for attention with what will be a 200-metre-high tower and another by Cesar Pelli (also under construction). Both towers configure all main facilities within a central core allowing open-plan floors throughout. While Foster's tower is given minimal expression through the curved corners of its sheer glass cladding, Pelli's glass-clad tower remains sharp at the corners.

The Citibank Headquarters is not as high-rise as its immediate neighbours but is more satisfying as a building. Located alongside the Jubilee Line station, it comprises two distinct parts: an office building to the west (17 floors above plaza level and four below) and a service core to the east (containing glass lifts, stairs, lavatories and mechanical and electrical services). The latter rises higher than the former in response to different height

Skidmore, Owings & Merrill, Inc. (masterplanners) 1988–2000

restrictions across the site. The two blocks are linked by glass-balustraded bridges to retain clarity of movement.

Tibbalds' fears about poor transport links to the development may have been assuaged, but as a model of urban design Canary Wharf still makes me shudder – I wonder about a place which requires such heavy policing by private security guards.

1 Cabot Square – Pei, Cobb, Freed & Partners
10 Cabot Square – Skidmore, Owings & Merrill, Inc.
20 Cabot Square – Kohn Pederson Fox
25 Cabot Square – Skidmore, Owings & Merrill, Inc.
25 The North Colonnade – Troughton McAslan
30 The South Colonnade – Kohn Pederson Fox
1 Canada Square/Cabot Place/Docklands Light Railway Station – Cesar Pelli & Associates

ADDRESS Isle of Dogs, London E14
DEVELOPER Olympia & York Canary Wharf Ltd
CONTRACT VALUE approximately £750 million
SIZE 28.3 hectares
TUBE Canary Wharf – Jubilee Line
DOCKLANDS LIGHT RAILWAY Canary Wharf
ACCESS restricted

Skidmore, Owings & Merrill, Inc. (masterplanners) 1988–2000

FLOATING BRIDGE

A tiny creature in the vast urban planes that are Docklands, the floating bridge provides a not as yet absolutely necessary link between Canary Wharf and an expansive, blustery-on-the-calmest-of-days promenade that stretches out in front of some derelict nine-teenth-century warehouses on West India Quay (presently under development) – a bridge from nowhere to nowhere. Actually, it is a footbridge: a lime-green, low, squat structure hovering on large padded feet like a waterboatman on a dockland millpond. Its ribbed sides bulge out as if flexed for a leap across to the next quay, with light-emitting handrails to show the way, rather like under-car lighting on a souped-up Ford Fiesta. Curiously, the architect states that 'colour is central to the concept' rather than the conveyance of pedestrians from one side of the water to the other. It nevertheless performs the latter task adequately enough without rising to the vertical challenge of its surroundings. However, if raised above the level of the DLR track entering Canary Wharf it might have afforded an unobstructed view eastwards of the Millennium Dome (see page 310).

ADDRESS north side of West India Quay, London E14
CLIENT London Docklands Development Corporation
STRUCTURAL ENGINEER Anthony Hunt Associates
SIZE 85-metre span
DOCKLANDS LIGHT RAILWAY Canary Wharf/West India Quay
ACCESS open

Future Systems 1994

THAMES BARRIER

DOCKLANDS AND THE GREENWICH PENINSULA

The need for this barrier arose from two main factors: the rise in the high-water level at London Bridge by about 750mm a century due to the melting of the polar ice caps; and the surge tides which originate as zones of atmospheric pressure off the coast of Canada. Where the warm Gulf Stream meets the cold Labrador Current the sea is raised around 300mm. This hump of water moves across the Atlantic and occasionally northerly winds force it down the North Sea, sending millions of tonnes of extra water up the Thames.

In 1970 the Greater London Council was given responsibility for the whole flood-prevention scheme. The width of the river is divided by piers to form six openings for shipping and four subsidiary non-navigational openings. Reinforced-concrete piers founded on coffer dams support a rotating circular arm to which are fixed the moon-shaped gates. The seating for the gates is provided by concrete sills, containing service ducts, which were cast, then sunk to the level of the chalk riverbed. The largest sill weighs 10,000 tonnes.

The gates themselves – four of 1500 tonnes and two of 750 tonnes – were manufactured at Darlington. These colossal elements had to be manoeuvred to within a maximum tolerance of 10mm, fixed by divers working in zero visibility. The upturned hull-shaped roofs not only act as the symbolic feature of the barrier above water level but also protect the operating machinery – reversible hydraulic rams that rotate the gates into any one of four positions. The roofs have timber shells covered with maintenance-free strips of stainless steel, which to this day gleam like medieval knights in shining armour.

ADDRESS Unity Way, London SE18
ENGINEER Rendel, Palmer & Tritton
RAIL Charlton
ACCESS telephone 020 8854 1373 for Visitors' Centre opening hours and boat cruises

GLC Department of Architecture 1984

THAMES BARRIER PARK

This is London's first major post-war park. It covers a previously contaminated brownfield site (once home to a chemical works and an armaments factory, among other things) on the north side of the river overlooking the mighty Thames Barrier. The site was no longer active after 1969 and between 1982–86 became an essential part of the then London Docklands Development Corporation's plan for the Royal Docks area – the largest urban regeneration project in the country. The result of an international design competition, this park's formal composition unites urban design, landscape, architecture and engineering to create a new and vital piece of infrastructure for the city. It has, in turn, generated a new enthusiasm for local development.

The uplifting design welcomes wide open surroundings – big skies, big feats of engineering and big possibilities. It comprises settings for different activities: approaching the park from the car park reminded me of walking up over sand dunes before reaching the beach. Here steps cut through an embankment of densely planted bamboo that makes an enchantingly soft rustling noise to counteract the grind of cars passing at high speed behind you. Once over the brow of this hill, visitors are greeted by a timber and glass café pavilion that overlooks the large, informal meadowed area of grassland and birch trees. A children's playground is to one side. A trench with 5-metre-high concrete walls slices diagonally through the park rather like a dry dock – a reminder of the scale and depth of former dockside structures. This device allows visitors to climb down into the sheltered 'rainbow gardens' with their carefully managed strips of colourful and fragrant planting or view them from above from one of the many bridges that traverse the so called 'Green Dock'.

The park culminates on the river's edge with a timber decked promenade and a place for contemplation beneath the Pavilion of Remembrance (commemorating the local

Patel Taylor with landscape architect Groupe Signes 2000

council's war dead). Its lofty timber slatted roof is held up on 23 spindly steel legs (like saplings in a forest clearing) sheltering low stone seating.

New housing developments now border the east and west sides of the park; more housing under construction to the north-east includes the construction of a primary school and shops. The proximity of this site to Canary Wharf, to amenities such as City Airport, the ExCel exhibition centre and the so-called 'Thames Gateway' with its Jubilee Line extension link from the centre of the City to Stratford in the east will make this area of London the focus of our attention for several years to come.

ADDRESS North Woolwich Road, Silvertown
CLIENT London Development Agency (LDA)
STRUCTURAL ENGINEER Arup
SIZE approximately 9 hectares
DOCKLANDS LIGHT RAILWAY Custom House

Patel Taylor with landscape architect Groupe Signes 2000

TRINITY BUOY WHARF

Not a particularly easy site to get to as the main roads are poorly signposted, but once you do reach the end of this spectacular peninsula at the mouth of Bow Creek with its unprecedented broad views of river activity and the Millennium Dome, you will be very glad you made the effort. And if you are interested in the resurgence of prefabricated construction methods (see also pages 186 and 246), this is an essential part of the tour.

Trinity Buoy Wharf is a centre for the arts and creative industries. The site was the subject of a competition held by the London Docklands Development Corporation and was won by the architects with their client to develop a series of projects known collectively as ContainerSpace. The concept explores the use (or re-use) of shipping containers to create low-cost flexible accommodation for a variety of functions. The container – redefined as a building type – sits happily in familiar surroundings.

Here Container City 1 (at the rear of the site) is a direct expression of the concept. The brief was to provide low-cost space for artists' studios. Several containers are grouped to form a cube with access provided via a vertical container accommodating a staircase. Container City 2 is more ambitious, creating a wider variety of shapes and sizes of workspace from under 20 square metres to 100 square metres with lift access mirroring the existing staircase. The arrangement is apparently more haphazard in order to create a colonnade between the two phases for vehicle deliveries and to provide shelter for pedestrians. The puzzle is trying to work out how far, and in which directions the 'city' can continue to grow.

These particular containers are entirely recycled. They are made of profiled steel with punched-out porthole windows and upgraded to provide high levels of thermal and acoustic insulation. Double doors at the ends of each unit are opened out to form fixed balconies. Each one is prefabricated off-site in a factory and then delivered on the back of

Nicholas Lacey & Partners 2001–02

TRINITY BUOY WHARF

a truck and craned into position, avoiding many of the problems associated with traditional building construction. The containers with their new coats of yellow, orange and red paint are a lively and optimistic addition to an area that no longer fulfills its original purpose as busy wharf.

The architects are currently developing the system to embrace other uses such as teaching space (ContainerLearn) and low-cost housing (ContainerHomes).

DOCKLANDS AND THE GREENWICH PENINSULA

ADDRESS Orchard Place, London E14
CLIENT Urban Space Management
SIZE 47 containers so far
DOCKLANDS LIGHT RAILWAY East India Dock
ACCESS restricted for individual studios

Nicholas Lacey & Partners 2001–02

BECKTON EXTENSION
DOCKLANDS LIGHT RAILWAY

Ten new stations have sprung up along an 8-kilometre stretch of land alongside Victoria Dock Road and the Royal Albert Dock Spine Road, extending the Docklands Light Railway to Beckton. Each uses a standard kit, designed to be both unified and flexible: to be identifiable as a route but able to accommodate different site conditions and station types including viaduct stations, island stations, stations built in the middle of roundabouts and the terminus. Staircases, lighting, canopies and lifts have been created on a modular system. Island stations (such as Prince Regent) and viaduct stations (such as Royal Albert) have cantilevered canopies supported by two sets of columns. A row of curved mullions extends from the main columns, spanning the tracks and then wrapped in a toughened glass skin. Electrical cabling is contained within the main columns. Lifts – clad in red vitreous enamel panels – are the only coloured element (all other steelwork blends into the silvery-grey dock landscape), punctured by portholes on each level and glazed on the top to emit a beacon light at night.

The one fundamental flaw in the scheme was the primary consideration for the design of the whole project. Cost-cutting disguised as the Docklands Light Railway 'streamlined service of the future' means that the stations are unmanned – can a light, transparent structure alone accommodate all the safety requirements of passengers?

CLIENTS London Docklands Development Corporation, Docklands Light Railway
STRUCTURAL ENGINEER The Maunsell Group
CONTRACT VALUE £280 million
ACCESS open during train-timetable hours

Ahrends Burton & Koralek 1994

DOCKLANDS AND THE GREENWICH PENINSULA

LONDON REGATTA CENTRE

The centre provides permanent facilities for local, national and international rowing activities organised by the Royal Albert Dock Trust. The site is located adjacent to the finishing line of the newly extended 2000-metre-long rowing course, providing south-east England with its first Olympic-standard rowing facility.

In response to the shape of the site, the centre has been conceived and planned as two separate buildings: a boathouse with ancillary workshop space, and a clubhouse with short-term accommodation for athletes. The clubhouse also has a unique rowing tank developed from a tenth-scale hydraulic model which uses flowing water to better simulate real open-water rowing.

The design strategy responds to the scale of the Royal Docks landscape by making a robust intervention capable of establishing a presence within a vast industrial wasteland. In this scheme gabion walls – a building technique (filling metal cages with rocks) more associated with civil engineering than architecture – are used to define spaces within which the buildings can nest. The boathouse is defined only by the freestanding gabion walls and a lightweight stiffened stainless-steel roof. The clubhouse sits back from the north-side gabion wall to create an access buffer zone spine running the length of the building. Terraces on the second level sail over the gabion to the south, providing areas from which to view racing events and the activities of the London City Airport.

ADDRESS Dockside Road, London E16
STRUCTURAL ENGINEER Ove Arup & Partners
SIZE both buildings 4350 square metres
DOCKLANDS LIGHT RAILWAY Royal Albert
ACCESS restricted

Ian Ritchie Architects 1999

UNIVERSITY OF EAST LONDON DOCKLANDS CAMPUS

UeL was formerly a polytechnic: with the modernisation of such establishments many have found it necessary to rebrand themselves. This project has provided an opportunity to be part of a much larger initiative to regenerate the whole area, as well as providing the centrepiece of the new university. Making use of a contaminated brownfield site, UeL – with London Guildhall University and Queen Mary and Westfield Colleges – is also developing The Thames Gateway Technology Centre to serve the business community in the region.

The campus is the first to be built in London for 50 years. The phase-one brief was for teaching and support accommodation for 2400 students in eight departments with the potential to grow within a masterplan eventually to accommodate 7000 students. Included in the plan are 28 business start-up units incorporated into the academic structure. In response to both the brief, which recommended a pedestrian square at the heart of the campus to create a social focus, and a very exposed site, the teaching blocks are arranged within a main colonnaded courtyard, providing shelter from the prevailing south-westerly wind and cold north-easterlies. Student accommodation is contained within the ten four-storey cylindrical blocks along the river frontage. The blocks are paired with the junction between each providing circulation. Each floor has five bedrooms grouped to one kitchen, all radiating from the centre of the plan to form wedge-shaped rooms. Most floors accommodate two such groups. Each bedroom contains its own factory-made shower/wc pod.

The teaching blocks were conceived as a 'white and silver cliff' expressed in an exposed steel frame hung with horizontal and vertical planes of white render to define floors and staircases respectively. The glazing is sandwiched between these planes, reinforcing the notion that the occupants of the site need protection from the elements. Inter-

Edward Cullinan Architects 1999/2000

nal streets within the blocks are naturally lit through rooflights. The steel structure juts out of the building envelope to frame the entrance of University Square, causing these inside/outside spaces to overlap each other. Colour is an important element of Cullinan's architectural form, used to distinguish areas of the campus: a red public face, yellow, blue and green student blocks.

It was intended that the project reflect best practice across the whole range of sustainable issues. This includes everything from encouraging students and staff to use the DLR or cycle to get to the site (parking space is limited) to crushing and reusing existing concrete pavements and structures as sub-base material, and cleaning contaminated sub-soil on site. The curved lintels on the windows of each student block were cast on site using the waste ready-mix concrete that would traditionally be skipped. The proximity to London City Airport means that the building cannot rely on natural ventilation: a Thermodeck hollow-core plank-floor system uses the structural slabs to distribute air and store energy within the building fabric. The energy consumption of the building is half the good-practice benchmark for higher-education buildings.

ADDRESS Royal Albert Way (north bank of Royal Albert Dock), London E16
STRUCTURAL ENGINEER Whitby Bird & Partners
LANDSCAPE ARCHITECT Livingstone Eyre
CONTRACT VALUE £33 million (first phase)
SIZE 19,000 square metres forming part of 10-hectare site
DOCKLANDS LIGHT RAILWAY Cyprus
ACCESS restricted

Edward Cullinan Architects 1999/2000

PEDESTRIAN BRIDGE AT ROYAL VICTORIA DOCK

The brief called for a covered pedestrian bridge to connect a yachting centre and housing development on the south bank of the dock with the Excel exhibition centre, new park, railway station and the City Airport on the north bank. It spans a distance of 130 metres and is elevated 15 metres above water on two piers. Commonly known as a transporter bridge, the type is familiar in industrial ports where the frequent passage of shipping might compromise an opening bridge. Here the type is reinterpreted to create an elegant, lightweight structure, accessed at either end by stair/elevator towers.

The structure is based on an inverted Fink truss that combines lightness with a very long span. The five box girders between the suspension members are raised in the middle and project through the timber decking. They are supported at each end by trestle legs. Six masts carry cables fixed along the length of the bridge; additional cables at either end carry tension forces down to the ground. The section of each element is carefully tuned to minimise the aerodynamic profile on this exposed site. The fully prestressed steel frame (prefabricated in sections sized to the limits of road transportation) was erected without bolting or welding – sections were connected with socket joints and fixed with cable stays.

It is immediately apparent that (in spite of the brief) the bridge provides no shelter – your passage is bracingly affected by weather. Phase two of the project proposes a glazed cabin to be hung beneath the deck (holding 40 people) and propelled along a cable mechanism in a parabolic curve like the inverted track of a cable car.

ADDRESS Royal Victoria Dock, off North Woolwich Road
STRUCTURAL ENGINEER Techniker
DOCKLANDS LIGHT RAILWAY Custom House
ACCESS open

Lifschutz Davidson 1998

THE GREENWICH PENINSULA

The Greenwich Peninsula was the focus of all our attention during 2000, not only as the home of the celebrations at the Millennium Dome, but also for the building programme that it has spawned. The first phase of the Greenwich Millennium Village as master-planned by Ralph Erskine is under construction (though two show homes are on permanent display on the site), while shopping is taken care of with the completion of a new Sainsbury's supermarket by Chetwood Associates. This area of south-east London, site of a former gasworks, is intended as a testing ground for prototypes.

The Millennium Experience at the Dome ran for one year as intended and closed on 31 December 2000 – at the time of writing its future is unknown. **THE MILLENNIUM DOME** (technically a tent), designed by the Richard Rogers Partnership, was no mean construction feat. Twelve masts are positioned around a 364-metre-diameter base, creating 80,000 square metres of floor area. The 90-metre-high masts, resting on 10-metre-high quadropods, support a grid of cables (using 67 kilometres of cable) which forms the domed cobweb (50 metres high at its apex). 150, 000 square metres of Teflon-coated glass-fibre fabric adheres to the cables to create an enclosure (big enough to house 18,000 double-decker buses). The risk of indoor rain clouds forming if condensation were to build up has been avoided by applying two layers of fabric for insulation. The largest fabric-covered structure of its kind ever made is unfortunately punctured by the ventilation tower (designed by Terry Farrell) for the Blackwall Tunnel.

The cost of the building is estimated at £54 million while the cost of cleaning up and developing the immediate surroundings is considerably higher at an estimated £750 million (provided by the National Lottery and private business). The Dome was the brainchild of a Conservative government in 1994. Despite protests from what was then the Labour Opposition, who saw the Dome as a symbolic temple of private enterprise, a

various architects

change in government in 1997 saw it adopted as a New Labour monument. The intense controversy over what would fill the structure was in design terms the most inelegant feature and politically the project's most revealing and subsequently disastrous aspect. The New Millennium Experience Company (a management body rather than a creative one) commissioned themed exhibitions ('zones'), each designed by a different architect or designer. They included The Mind Zone by Zaha Hadid, The Faith Zone by Eva Jiricna Architects, The Body Zone by Branson Coates, and the Learning Zone by Allford Hall Monaghan Morris.

As an event, or rather – as the advertising campaign described it – 'One Great Day', it was an unmitigated disaster – a direct result of having had absolutely no singular coherent vision. The experience was akin to being thrust into the world's largest food court with appropriate aromas to hyper-realise the moment. Any notion of how to accommodate/entertain/interest large crowds of people of different ages was fundamentally misunderstood. It was more an exercise in how to control/placate/baffle. If attendance ever reached the expected figures long queues formed at each exhibition and visitors bore the expressions of those awaiting an uncertain fate. The exhibitions themselves were glorified trade-show stands. However, the lasting feature of the Dome is the main structure itself, made even more elegant by the fact that all 1800 tonnes of it weighs less than the air inside. Whoever becomes its next tenant would do well to make the most of the vast volume of covered space as a whole rather than treating it as another National Exhibition Centre.

In 1997 deputy prime minister John Prescott launched the 13-hectare **GREENWICH MILLENNIUM VILLAGE** site:

> I want to create a number of residential communities on the Greenwich Peninsula that will
> represent best practice in creating a sustainable urban environment. This competition
> provides a golden opportunity to create a legacy for the future – a living community for
> a new Millennium.

A competition for a masterplan was run by English Partnerships (EP –the government's regeneration agency) with Countryside Properties and Taylor Woodrow, and won by Ralph Erskine with HTA Architects. A second phase has been designed by Proctor Matthews. EP promised a 'showpiece of world-leading environmental sustainability, 80 per cent reduction in energy consumption and 30 per cent reduction in water usage, with phase one to be built in time for the millennium celebrations'. However, the project has been hampered from the outset. Planning negotiations delayed the start of the project by a year; EP agreed that the targets for build costs, build time and energy use would be reduced and HTA walked off the scheme, claiming innovation had been watered down.

In the meantime the nearby **SAINSBURY'S** by Chetwood Associates has attracted more than its fair share of attention (much more than a supermarket that boasts a huge open-air forecourt carpark and claims to be a prototype low-energy store deserves). The store was designed to overcome the two major flaws in the supermarket/superstore building type, i.e., windowless and therefore artificially lit sheds. The wind turbines declare the intentions of the project (in fact they provide enough power to light the sign above the entrance). A timber-clad façade and grass roof make the customer feel good

various architects

about themselves entering the store. The interior space is elevated by a single 26-metre-span barrel vault, with north-light glazing. The thrust of the arched roof beams is resisted by heavy concrete walls along the sides of the building and backed by earth fill which also gives thermal mass to the structure (it is a useful grass roof).

The architects claim that there is a 50 per cent reduction in energy use as a result of recycling the heat generated by the propane-based refrigeration system. 70-metre bore-holes enable warm air to push up naturally through vents in the floor without recourse to air conditioning. The shape acts as a heat sink, allowing energy to be stored under the insulated turf roof. Rainwater is recycled as grey water for sanitary purposes and watering the garden, cleaned through reed beds. Overall this amounts to savings of about £75,000 per annum for an outlay of some 25 per cent more than a conventional building. Yet none of these features is expressed through the architecture. Token gestures such as the splashbacks in the WCs made from recycled yoghurt cartons are not a sufficient justification for the unquantifiable waste that is the store's by-product once customers have got their loot home.

ADDRESS approach from Blackwall Lane, London SE10
TUBE North Greenwich – Jubilee Line
ACCESS restricted in housing areas

various architects

GREENWICH MILLENNIUM VILLAGE SCHOOL AND HEALTH CENTRE

Three interconnected buildings for health, education and the community quietly mark the entrance to the new village next to the Dome. Ralph Erskine's masterplan prescribed that all buildings should be close to and framing the pedestrian and cycle routes that cross the area. The need to reuse waste heat and water and specify building components with the potential for reuse and recycling all helped to shape design intentions.

The rippling walls of the primary school, the school hall (which also serves as a public hall) and health centre are grouped to face south over gardens and playgrounds. Beyond is an all-weather football pitch and badminton court surrounded by landscaped hills made from recycled site material. The uses of these buildings have been extended to include an after-hours school club, crèche and early years centre, drama and music school and open-learning centre for adults. The buildings are fully glazed with shading on their south elevations to maximise passive solar gain. Perimeter walls are wrapped in vertical English larch boards with intermittent slots of glazing. The effect is more fortress than joyful display of civic amenities.

Energy savings are achieved through very high levels of insulation, natural lighting wherever possible, heating and ventilation through hollow concrete floors, rainwater storage, and the use of materials that either store energy or use little in their production and installation. Limited parking is provided to encourage use of the tube and river bus-links. But what undermines the approach is that the closest grocery shop is a superstore.

ADDRESS Health Centre, Schoolbank Road/School, 50 John Harrison Way London SE10
STRUCTURAL ENGINEER Price & Myers **M&E ENGINEER** Fulcrum Consulting
TUBE North Greenwich – Jubilee Line
ACCESS restricted access to both; the privacy of patients and pupils must be respected

Edward Cullinan Architects 2000

JUBILEE LINE EXTENSION

JUBILEE LINE EXTENSION

In 1993 the chairman of London Transport, Sir Wilfred Newton, invited Roland Paoletti to head a team which would establish – very quickly – a Jubilee Line Extension (JLE) for the London Underground. Paoletti, had worked for the previous 15 years on the new metro system in Hong Kong. He knew immediately how he would approach the scheme and which architects he would commission to design the six new stations and to remodel and modernise another five. Architects were chosen for their ability to design from first principles; most were younger practices with little or no experience in this field but who showed engineering to be fundamental to their architecture. The use of different architects for each site reinforced the notion of an extension – that is, the task was not to design an entirely new transport system that would be a model for future lines but to celebrate the existing system and its expansion. And as each site presented different conditions and requirements, employing different teams ensured that the architects would define each task anew.

The JLE provides an underground link between central London and the east via the south of the river and Docklands. The most important addition to the London Underground (LU) network in 25 years has been 50 years in the planning, and the history of the transport studies that underlie the various routes considered is a book in itself – *Extending the Jubilee Line: The Planning Story* by Jon Willis. The route was decided in 1990, and following Paoletti's appointment in 1993 the commissioned architects had just two years to complete their designs. The only givens were the widths of the platforms and tracks. The first principles for the design of each station, as laid out by Paoletti, were driven by what he sees as the currently pitiful state of LU (he does not accept the argument that no money equals poor quality) and inspired by his own background in structural architecture (he was a pupil of Pier Luigi Nervi). The design priorities included generous and easily understood space with as much daylight as possible to generate a sense of ease; clear and direct passenger routing; escalators in minimum banks of three; plenty of lifts (there are 188 along the extension – double the number in the whole of the rest of the LU, although many of them need to be operated on request by staff); abundant protected escape routes; and platform-edge glazed screens (the first in the UK) at stations between Westminster and North Greenwich.

Given the vastness of the project and the fact that the architects were employed on design-and-build contracts (handing over supervision of construction and finishes to a separate team of civil engineers at each site), Paoletti encouraged them to produce simple raw spaces and structures without elaborate finishes. The principles of stage lighting are employed to manipulate scale and create atmosphere: house lighting throughout, with spotlights on specific features and a mixture of spot and scenery lighting for maximum dramatic effect. Prioritising the idea that the stations should perform their function spatially, and not ashamed to say they may appear a little rough and ready, Paoletti quotes Louis Kahn: 'The right thing done badly is better than the wrong thing done well'.

Three methods of construction were used to build the stations and two main tunnelling systems dealt with specific ground conditions. New platforms and tunnels at **LONDON BRIDGE** (Jubilee Line Extension Architects and Weston Williamson), already London's busiest interchange, and **WATERLOO** (Jubilee Line Extension Architects), an international interchange, called for underground mining and excavation of London clay. Huge caverns were created using the New Austrian Tunnelling Method (NATM), which as it digs sprays a thin layer of quick-setting concrete on to the walls, to be reinforced later with steel mesh and more concrete.

Westminster, Southwark and Bermondsey are combined open-cut boxes (like open-heart surgery) with mined tunnels to platform levels. **WESTMINSTER** (Michael Hopkins & Partners) was the most complex and restricted work site on a very deep section of the line. An entirely new station box replaces the Victorian structure, revealing an open-plan escalator well combined with the foundation for Portcullis House (by the same architect; see pages 70–72), above ground – all constructed in close proximity to landmark buildings while keeping existing lines running. The breathtaking vertical decent to platform level is like travelling backwards and upside-down, inside an underground skyscraper – the vast lateral bracing holding the walls apart for passengers to flow between. Consistent cool lighting reflected off of the smooth concrete wall surfaces counteracts any feeling of subterranean gloom.

The construction of a new interchange with Waterloo East's mainline services at **SOUTHWARK** (MacCormac Jamieson Prichard; picture on page 323) was dominated by a fragile viaduct nearby. Earth and building movements were monitored by computer and any slumps dealt with by compensation grouting (this method of shoring-up weak areas of earth by injecting strands of grout was used throughout the project). The station is an assemblage of concourses connected by escalators. The drum-shaped main ticket hall on Blackfriars Road was designed to accommodate a 14-storey building above (as yet unbuilt). Its gently domed ceiling deliberately recalls the Holden stations of the 1930s. An intermediate concourse connects the main ticket hall with access from Waterloo East. The pivotal space is defined by the 'elliptical cone' wall made of triangular panes of blue enamelled glass designed in collaboration with artist Alexander Beleschenko and structural engineers Adams Kara Taylor. Opposite this is a straight polished-concrete wall with three gaping arched entrances to escalators descending to platforms a further two levels below.

At **BERMONDSEY** (Ian Ritchie Architects; picture on page 325) natural light is

exploited by providing a translucent roof like a glass lid over the main concourse. A three-dimensional grid of smooth concrete columns and lateral bracing grows out of the lower levels and up towards the daylight, rejoicing in its lack of adornment. This is the area's first Underground station.

Canada Water, Canary Wharf and North Greenwich are large, open-box, cut-and-cover structures with 140-metre-long platforms built into the bottom levels. The only visible signs of a station at **CANADA WATER** (Jubilee Line Extension Architects) are a shallow glass drum and a triangular ventilation shaft; the rest of its mass (comparable in size to St Paul's Cathedral) is 23 metres below the surface.

The open box at **CANARY WHARF** (Foster and Partners; picture on page 327) measures 280 metres long and 32 metres wide (large enough to encase the Canary Wharf tower on its side) and is 24 metres below pavement level. 160,000 tonnes of water were drained from West India Quay to create a dry bed for the station. This is predicted to be the busiest station at peak times on the network, and verges on the magnificent. Above ground three shallow stingray-shaped glass canopies mark entrances at either end of the landscaped garden which forms the roof over the main ticket hall below. Passengers are swallowed by 20 banks of escalators to be absorbed like tiny specks of plankton into the belly of this whale. All offices, kiosks and other amenities are located along the side walls behind stainless-steel panels leaving the ticket hall volume free except for a central row of elliptical columns. Platforms lie one level below, still benefiting from the daylight drawn in by the roof canopies. Simple, hard-wearing and easily maintained materials enhance the spatial sensation.

NORTH GREENWICH (Alsop Lyall & Störmer & Jubilee Line Extension Architects), the world's largest underground station, is 405 metres long and 32 metres wide, and

required the removal of 300,000 cubic metres of spoil. During 2000 it provided the main transport link to the Millennium Dome. Strangely, the ground-level enclosure was designed by Norman Foster & Partners. More subaqua than subterranean, the main concourse rests in the ground like the hulking hull of a docked ship, suspended just above the tracks with views down to and up from the platforms on either side. The roof is supported by 21 pairs of 13-metre-high sloping columns. The station's structure is held down simply by its own weight. Different types of cladding surface are all saturated in a deep underwater blue.

Canning Town, West Ham and Stratford are all multi-level stations. At **CANNING TOWN** (Troughton McAslan) an underground concourse supports six tracks and three platforms. The Docklands Light Railway tracks are elevated above the Jubilee Line and the below-ground platforms link to the ground-level North London Line and new bus station. At **WEST HAM** (Van Heyningen & Haward) an existing station has been completely redesigned. A horizontal building made up of red- and glass-brick corridors bridges three railway lines and a major road. It is the only joyless moment on the route.

STRATFORD, the grand terminus (picture on page 329), is the work of two different teams. Troughton McAslan designed the platforms and accommodation building; the 'breaking wave' that is the distinctive concourse building is by Chris Wilkinson Architects. The station is at surface level and the concourse building provides an interchange between five different railway lines and the bus station. The sweep of the curved roof breaks over a sloping glass screen wall that faces towards the town centre and the Jubilee Line; all other sides of the building are also glazed to provide clear views out to other lines and to maximise daylight and natural ventilation. A mezzanine level provides direct access to the mainline railway with the lower level concourse serving the underground

lines. Sheltered seating areas made from ceramic-faced blockwork and covered by wing-shaped aluminium canopies are located along the new platforms.

A project of this size inevitably encounters practical problems. One of the biggest was the collapse of the sprayed-concrete NATM tunnels at Heathrow, which (although not directly associated with the JLE) halted work until the system could be proved safe. The scale and complexity of the construction, particularly in areas where Underground services had to be maintained, led to overspending. In parallel with this are the scale and complexity of co-ordinating separate civil-engineering and electrical-engineering contracts at each site, with up to 15 different contractors working simultaneously. A crucial question is whether London Transport will maintain the stations (which have been designed to last a hundred years) to a high standard. The new mayor must insist on it.

No one would have ever predicted that travelling on the London Underground could be as uplifting, intriguing and as literally transporting as a journey on the JLE has proved. But what long-term effect will the JLE have on the map of central London? A small research team at the University of Westminster has devised a data-collection programme to provide transport planners with information about the impact of such proposals. The benefits of the link will inform future decisions about the proposed Crossrail route from Stratford to Paddington (en route for Heathrow), a Chelsea/Hackney Line and the Thames Gateway Metro. All of these would not only significantly reduce road traffic and make for a more efficient metropolitan transport system, but could provide architects with the challenge of creating another kind of architecture for the city.

INDEX

LONDON: A GUIDE TO RECENT ARCHITECTURE